TEACHER'S PET PUBLICATIONS

PUZZLE PACK
for
And Then There Were None
based on the book by
Agatha Christie

Written by
Mary B. Collins

© 2008 Teacher's Pet Publications
All Rights Reserved

The materials in this packet are copyrighted
by Teacher's Pet Publications, Inc.

These pages may be duplicated by the purchaser
for use in the purchaser's own classroom.

Copying any of these materials and distributing them
for any other purpose is a violation of the copyright laws.

© 2008 Teacher's Pet Publications, Inc.
www.tpet.com

INTRODUCTION
If you already own the LitPlan for this title, this Puzzle Pack will refresh your Unit Resource Materials and Vocabulary Resource Materials sections plus give you additional materials you can substitute into the tests. If you do not already have a complete LitPlan, these pages will give you some supplemental materials to use with your own plan. There are two main groups of materials: one set for unit words (such as characters' names, symbols, places, etc.) and one set for vocabulary words associated with the book.

WORD LIST
There is a word list for both the unit words and the vocabulary words. These lists show you which words are being used in the materials and the clues or definitions being used for those words. You may want to give students a word list with clues/definitions to help them, or you may want students to only have a word list (without clues/definitions) if you want them to work a little harder. Both are available for duplication. The word lists can also be your "calling key" for the bingo games.

FILL IN THE BLANK AND MATCHING
There are 4 each of the fill in the blank and matching worksheets for both the unit and vocabulary words. These pages can be used either as extra worksheets for students or as objective parts of a unit test. They can be done individually if students need extra help or as a whole class activity to review the material covered.

MAGIC SQUARES
The magic squares not only reinforce the material covered but also work on reasoning and math skills. Many teachers have told us that their students really enjoy doing these!

WORD SEARCH PUZZLES
The word search words go in all directions, as indicated on your answer keys. Two of the word search puzzles have the clues listed rather than the words. This makes the puzzle a little more difficult, but it reinforces the material better. Two word search puzzles have words only for students who find the clue puzzles too difficult.

CROSSWORD PUZZLES
Both unit and vocabulary word sections have 4 crossword puzzles.

BINGO CARDS
There are 32 individual bingo cards for the unit words and 32 individual bingo cards for the vocabulary words. You can use your word list as a "call list," calling the words at random and marking them off of your list as you go, or you could use the flash cards by cutting them apart and drawing the words at random from a hat (or box or whatever). To make a better review, you might ask for the definition and spelling of each word as you call it out–or you could call out the definitions and have students tell you the words they need to look for on the puzzle.

JUGGLE LETTERS
The vocabulary juggle letter game is intended to help students learn the spellings of the words. One sheet has the definitions listed on it as an extra help for students who need it or to reinforce the definitions if you choose to do so.

FLASH CARDS
We've included a set of vocabulary flash cards you can duplicate, cut, and fold for your students. Some teachers make a few sets for general use by the class; others make a set for each student. Some teachers duplicate them for each student and have the students cut & fold their own. You can cut out just the words and put them in a hat, have each student pick out one word and write the definition and a sentence for that word. Students then swap words and papers, with the next student adding a sentence of his own under the last one. You can have students swap as many times as you like. Each time the student will read the sentences written prior to his own and then add a sentence. You can cut out the words and definitions separately and play "I Have; Who Has?" Each student in the room draws a word and definition. The first student says, "I have (the name of the word). Who has the definition?" The student with the definition reads it then says, "I have (the name of the vocabulary word she has). Who has the definition?" The round continues until all words and definitions have been given.

And Then There Were None Word List

No.	Word	Clue/Definition
1.	ARTHUR	Had an affair with his friend's wife
2.	AXE	Rogers was killed with this.
3.	BEACH	Where Armstrong's body was found
4.	BEAR	The marble clock was in this shape
5.	BEATRICE	Drowned herself after becoming pregnant
6.	BEE	Emily noticed one on the dining room window.
7.	BLORE	Committed perjury which led to the death of an innocent man
8.	BLUDGEONING	General Macarthur's cause of death
9.	BOAT	The guests anxiously awaited its arrival, but it never came.
10.	BOTTLE	A fisherman found the confession in this.
11.	BRADY	Died after necessary medicine was withheld
12.	BUTLER	Job of Mr. Rogers
13.	CHRISTIE	Author of And Then There Were None
14.	CLAYTHORNE	Vera's last name
15.	CLEES	Died on the operating table
16.	CLOCK	Blore was killed with this item.
17.	COMBES	Was run down by a reckless driver
18.	CYRIL	Drowned when allowed to swim too far out to sea
19.	DAVIS	Mr. Blore's assumed name when he arrived on the island
20.	EMILY	Led someone to suicide through moral judgment
21.	ENGLAND	Country in which the story takes place
22.	HANGING	Vera's means of death
23.	HERRING	False clue in a murder mystery: a red ___
24.	HOOK	Vera noticed this in the ceiling near her bed.
25.	HUGO	Knew that murder had been committed to win his love
26.	INDIAN	Ten of these figures were on the table in the beginning.
27.	ISLAND	Setting of the novel: Indian ___
28.	JUDGE	Wargrave's occupation
29.	KNITTING	Emily's pastime
30.	LITTLE	Original title: Ten ___ Indians
31.	LOMBARD	Abandoned a group of men under attack
32.	MACARTHUR	Killed someone for sleeping with his wife
33.	MARSTON	Killed someone by being too reckless
34.	MORRIS	Conducted the purchase of Indian Island for an unnamed third party
35.	MURDER	The voice accused each of the guests of this.
36.	NARRACOTT	Captain of the boat that took the guests to the island
37.	NURSERY	The murders followed the ___ rhyme.
38.	OILSILK	This curtain was missing from the bathroom.
39.	OWEN	Supposed owner of the island: Mr. U. N. ___
40.	PHILLIP	Mr. Lombard's first name
41.	POE	Credited as inventor of murder mystery genre
42.	POISON	Marston's cause of death
43.	REVOLVER	Lombard brought this weapon to the island.
44.	ROGERS	Killed an employer by withholding medicine
45.	SECRETARY	Vera's hired position with Mrs. Owen
46.	SETON	Wargrave cooked HIS goose.
47.	SWAN	Title of the song on the gramophone: ___ Song
48.	SYRINGE	Armstrong was missing this item from his bag.
49.	TAYLOR	Beatrice's last name
50.	TONGUE	The group was reduced to eating this.

And Then There Were None Word List Cont.

No.	Word	Clue/Definition
51.	TORTOISE	Wargrave was said to look like a wary old one of these.
52.	VERA	Allowed a weak young boy to drown
53.	WARGRAVE	Famous for making harsh judgments
54.	YARN	Emily was missing it, and it turned up on the judge.

And Then There Were None Fill In The Blanks 1

_____ 1. False clue in a murder mystery: a red ___

_____ 2. A fisherman found the confession in this.

_____ 3. The guests anxiously awaited its arrival, but it never came.

_____ 4. Drowned when allowed to swim too far out to sea

_____ 5. The murders followed the ___ rhyme.

_____ 6. Beatrice's last name

_____ 7. Died on the operating table

_____ 8. Emily noticed one on the dining room window.

_____ 9. Setting of the novel: Indian ___

_____ 10. Captain of the boat that took the guests to the island

_____ 11. Wargrave cooked HIS goose.

_____ 12. Vera's means of death

_____ 13. Knew that murder had been committed to win his love

_____ 14. Supposed owner of the island: Mr. U. N. ___

_____ 15. Killed someone by being too reckless

_____ 16. Armstrong was missing this item from his bag.

_____ 17. Committed perjury which led to the death of an innocent man

_____ 18. Where Armstrong's body was found

_____ 19. Famous for making harsh judgments

_____ 20. Was run down by a reckless driver

And Then There Were None Fill In The Blanks 1 Answer Key

Answer	Clue
HERRING	1. False clue in a murder mystery: a red ___
BOTTLE	2. A fisherman found the confession in this.
BOAT	3. The guests anxiously awaited its arrival, but it never came.
CYRIL	4. Drowned when allowed to swim too far out to sea
NURSERY	5. The murders followed the ___ rhyme.
TAYLOR	6. Beatrice's last name
CLEES	7. Died on the operating table
BEE	8. Emily noticed one on the dining room window.
ISLAND	9. Setting of the novel: Indian ___
NARRACOTT	10. Captain of the boat that took the guests to the island
SETON	11. Wargrave cooked HIS goose.
HANGING	12. Vera's means of death
HUGO	13. Knew that murder had been committed to win his love
OWEN	14. Supposed owner of the island: Mr. U. N. ___
MARSTON	15. Killed someone by being too reckless
SYRINGE	16. Armstrong was missing this item from his bag.
BLORE	17. Committed perjury which led to the death of an innocent man
BEACH	18. Where Armstrong's body was found
WARGRAVE	19. Famous for making harsh judgments
COMBES	20. Was run down by a reckless driver

And Then There Were None Fill In The Blanks 2

_____ 1. Famous for making harsh judgments
_____ 2. Where Armstrong's body was found
_____ 3. Ten of these figures were on the table in the beginning.
_____ 4. The group was reduced to eating this.
_____ 5. Blore was killed with this item.
_____ 6. Killed an employer by withholding medicine
_____ 7. Led someone to suicide through moral judgment
_____ 8. Mr. Blore's assumed name when he arrived on the island
_____ 9. Job of Mr. Rogers
_____ 10. The marble clock was in this shape
_____ 11. Title of the song on the gramophone: ___ Song
_____ 12. Committed perjury which led to the death of an innocent man
_____ 13. Country in which the story takes place
_____ 14. Marston's cause of death
_____ 15. Wargrave cooked HIS goose.
_____ 16. Captain of the boat that took the guests to the island
_____ 17. Credited as inventor of murder mystery genre
_____ 18. The murders followed the ___ rhyme.
_____ 19. Wargrave's occupation
_____ 20. Vera's means of death

And Then There Were None Fill In The Blanks 2 Answer Key

WARGRAVE	1. Famous for making harsh judgments
BEACH	2. Where Armstrong's body was found
INDIAN	3. Ten of these figures were on the table in the beginning.
TONGUE	4. The group was reduced to eating this.
CLOCK	5. Blore was killed with this item.
ROGERS	6. Killed an employer by withholding medicine
EMILY	7. Led someone to suicide through moral judgment
DAVIS	8. Mr. Blore's assumed name when he arrived on the island
BUTLER	9. Job of Mr. Rogers
BEAR	10. The marble clock was in this shape
SWAN	11. Title of the song on the gramophone: ___ Song
BLORE	12. Committed perjury which led to the death of an innocent man
ENGLAND	13. Country in which the story takes place
POISON	14. Marston's cause of death
SETON	15. Wargrave cooked HIS goose.
NARRACOTT	16. Captain of the boat that took the guests to the island
POE	17. Credited as inventor of murder mystery genre
NURSERY	18. The murders followed the ___ rhyme.
JUDGE	19. Wargrave's occupation
HANGING	20. Vera's means of death

And Then There Were None Fill In The Blanks 3

_____   1. Vera's means of death
_____   2. Emily was missing it, and it turned up on the judge.
_____   3. Killed someone for sleeping with his wife
_____   4. Abandoned a group of men under attack
_____   5. Lombard brought this weapon to the island.
_____   6. Emily noticed one on the dining room window.
_____   7. Had an affair with his friend's wife
_____   8. Was run down by a reckless driver
_____   9. The murders followed the ___ rhyme.
_____ 10. Wargrave was said to look like a wary old one of these.
_____ 11. Emily's pastime
_____ 12. Setting of the novel: Indian ___
_____ 13. Mr. Lombard's first name
_____ 14. Wargrave cooked HIS goose.
_____ 15. Vera noticed this in the ceiling near her bed.
_____ 16. Title of the song on the gramophone: ___ Song
_____ 17. Drowned herself after becoming pregnant
_____ 18. Committed perjury which led to the death of an innocent man
_____ 19. Credited as inventor of murder mystery genre
_____ 20. Killed an employer by withholding medicine

And Then There Were None Fill In The Blanks 3 Answer Key

HANGING	1. Vera's means of death
YARN	2. Emily was missing it, and it turned up on the judge.
MACARTHUR	3. Killed someone for sleeping with his wife
LOMBARD	4. Abandoned a group of men under attack
REVOLVER	5. Lombard brought this weapon to the island.
BEE	6. Emily noticed one on the dining room window.
ARTHUR	7. Had an affair with his friend's wife
COMBES	8. Was run down by a reckless driver
NURSERY	9. The murders followed the ___ rhyme.
TORTOISE	10. Wargrave was said to look like a wary old one of these.
KNITTING	11. Emily's pastime
ISLAND	12. Setting of the novel: Indian ___
PHILLIP	13. Mr. Lombard's first name
SETON	14. Wargrave cooked HIS goose.
HOOK	15. Vera noticed this in the ceiling near her bed.
SWAN	16. Title of the song on the gramophone: ___ Song
BEATRICE	17. Drowned herself after becoming pregnant
BLORE	18. Committed perjury which led to the death of an innocent man
POE	19. Credited as inventor of murder mystery genre
ROGERS	20. Killed an employer by withholding medicine

And Then There Were None Fill In The Blanks 4

_____ 1. Mr. Lombard's first name

_____ 2. Wargrave's occupation

_____ 3. Title of the song on the gramophone: ___ Song

_____ 4. Vera's means of death

_____ 5. The marble clock was in this shape

_____ 6. Knew that murder had been committed to win his love

_____ 7. The murders followed the ___ rhyme.

_____ 8. The voice accused each of the guests of this.

_____ 9. Killed someone for sleeping with his wife

_____ 10. Supposed owner of the island: Mr. U. N. ___

_____ 11. Vera's hired position with Mrs. Owen

_____ 12. Ten of these figures were on the table in the beginning.

_____ 13. A fisherman found the confession in this.

_____ 14. Conducted the purchase of Indian Island for an unnamed third party

_____ 15. Committed perjury which led to the death of an innocent man

_____ 16. Died after necessary medicine was withheld

_____ 17. Mr. Blore's assumed name when he arrived on the island

_____ 18. Armstrong was missing this item from his bag.

_____ 19. Killed someone by being too reckless

_____ 20. The group was reduced to eating this.

And Then There Were None Fill In The Blanks 4 Answer Key

PHILLIP	1. Mr. Lombard's first name
JUDGE	2. Wargrave's occupation
SWAN	3. Title of the song on the gramophone: ___ Song
HANGING	4. Vera's means of death
BEAR	5. The marble clock was in this shape
HUGO	6. Knew that murder had been committed to win his love
NURSERY	7. The murders followed the ___ rhyme.
MURDER	8. The voice accused each of the guests of this.
MACARTHUR	9. Killed someone for sleeping with his wife
OWEN	10. Supposed owner of the island: Mr. U. N. ___
SECRETARY	11. Vera's hired position with Mrs. Owen
INDIAN	12. Ten of these figures were on the table in the beginning.
BOTTLE	13. A fisherman found the confession in this.
MORRIS	14. Conducted the purchase of Indian Island for an unnamed third party
BLORE	15. Committed perjury which led to the death of an innocent man
BRADY	16. Died after necessary medicine was withheld
DAVIS	17. Mr. Blore's assumed name when he arrived on the island
SYRINGE	18. Armstrong was missing this item from his bag.
MARSTON	19. Killed someone by being too reckless
TONGUE	20. The group was reduced to eating this.

And Then There Were None Matching 1

___ 1. SETON   A. Marston's cause of death
___ 2. ARTHUR   B. Knew that murder had been committed to win his love
___ 3. CHRISTIE   C. Mr. Blore's assumed name when he arrived on the island
___ 4. POISON   D. Allowed a weak young boy to drown
___ 5. CLAYTHORNE   E. Armstrong was missing this item from his bag.
___ 6. HOOK   F. Lombard brought this weapon to the island.
___ 7. SYRINGE   G. Where Armstrong's body was found
___ 8. HUGO   H. Emily noticed one on the dining room window.
___ 9. MACARTHUR   I. Beatrice's last name
___10. MARSTON   J. Title of the song on the gramophone: ___ Song
___11. JUDGE   K. Vera noticed this in the ceiling near her bed.
___12. EMILY   L. Job of Mr. Rogers
___13. PHILLIP   M. Killed someone by being too reckless
___14. REVOLVER   N. Wargrave cooked HIS goose.
___15. BUTLER   O. Mr. Lombard's first name
___16. DAVIS   P. Had an affair with his friend's wife
___17. ENGLAND   Q. Author of And Then There Were None
___18. VERA   R. Killed someone for sleeping with his wife
___19. BOTTLE   S. Setting of the novel: Indian ___
___20. HERRING   T. Vera's last name
___21. BEACH   U. A fisherman found the confession in this.
___22. TAYLOR   V. Country in which the story takes place
___23. SWAN   W. Led someone to suicide through moral judgment
___24. BEE   X. False clue in a murder mystery: a red ___
___25. ISLAND   Y. Wargrave's occupation

And Then There Were None Matching 1 Answer Key

N - 1.	SETON	A.	Marston's cause of death
P - 2.	ARTHUR	B.	Knew that murder had been committed to win his love
Q - 3.	CHRISTIE	C.	Mr. Blore's assumed name when he arrived on the island
A - 4.	POISON	D.	Allowed a weak young boy to drown
T - 5.	CLAYTHORNE	E.	Armstrong was missing this item from his bag.
K - 6.	HOOK	F.	Lombard brought this weapon to the island.
E - 7.	SYRINGE	G.	Where Armstrong's body was found
B - 8.	HUGO	H.	Emily noticed one on the dining room window.
R - 9.	MACARTHUR	I.	Beatrice's last name
M -10.	MARSTON	J.	Title of the song on the gramophone: ___ Song
Y -11.	JUDGE	K.	Vera noticed this in the ceiling near her bed.
W -12.	EMILY	L.	Job of Mr. Rogers
O -13.	PHILLIP	M.	Killed someone by being too reckless
F -14.	REVOLVER	N.	Wargrave cooked HIS goose.
L -15.	BUTLER	O.	Mr. Lombard's first name
C -16.	DAVIS	P.	Had an affair with his friend's wife
V -17.	ENGLAND	Q.	Author of And Then There Were None
D -18.	VERA	R.	Killed someone for sleeping with his wife
U -19.	BOTTLE	S.	Setting of the novel: Indian ___
X -20.	HERRING	T.	Vera's last name
G -21.	BEACH	U.	A fisherman found the confession in this.
I -22.	TAYLOR	V.	Country in which the story takes place
J -23.	SWAN	W.	Led someone to suicide through moral judgment
H -24.	BEE	X.	False clue in a murder mystery: a red ___
S -25.	ISLAND	Y.	Wargrave's occupation

And Then There Were None Matching 2

___ 1. NURSERY   A. The murders followed the ___ rhyme.
___ 2. SETON   B. Ten of these figures were on the table in the beginning.
___ 3. EMILY   C. Famous for making harsh judgments
___ 4. LOMBARD   D. Vera's means of death
___ 5. MORRIS   E. Vera's hired position with Mrs. Owen
___ 6. CYRIL   F. Led someone to suicide through moral judgment
___ 7. MACARTHUR   G. Was run down by a reckless driver
___ 8. SYRINGE   H. This curtain was missing from the bathroom.
___ 9. VERA   I. Wargrave cooked HIS goose.
___10. CLAYTHORNE   J. Allowed a weak young boy to drown
___11. PHILLIP   K. Conducted the purchase of Indian Island for an unnamed third party
___12. OILSILK   L. General Macarthur's cause of death
___13. BEACH   M. Drowned when allowed to swim too far out to sea
___14. WARGRAVE   N. Abandoned a group of men under attack
___15. REVOLVER   O. Emily noticed one on the dining room window.
___16. COMBES   P. Armstrong was missing this item from his bag.
___17. DAVIS   Q. Had an affair with his friend's wife
___18. INDIAN   R. Vera's last name
___19. BLUDGEONING   S. Where Armstrong's body was found
___20. BEE   T. Killed someone for sleeping with his wife
___21. CLOCK   U. Lombard brought this weapon to the island.
___22. SECRETARY   V. Blore was killed with this item.
___23. HANGING   W. Drowned herself after becoming pregnant
___24. BEATRICE   X. Mr. Lombard's first name
___25. ARTHUR   Y. Mr. Blore's assumed name when he arrived on the island

And Then There Were None Matching 2 Answer Key

A - 1. NURSERY	A. The murders followed the ___ rhyme.
I - 2. SETON	B. Ten of these figures were on the table in the beginning.
F - 3. EMILY	C. Famous for making harsh judgments
N - 4. LOMBARD	D. Vera's means of death
K - 5. MORRIS	E. Vera's hired position with Mrs. Owen
M - 6. CYRIL	F. Led someone to suicide through moral judgment
T - 7. MACARTHUR	G. Was run down by a reckless driver
P - 8. SYRINGE	H. This curtain was missing from the bathroom.
J - 9. VERA	I. Wargrave cooked HIS goose.
R - 10. CLAYTHORNE	J. Allowed a weak young boy to drown
X - 11. PHILLIP	K. Conducted the purchase of Indian Island for an unnamed third party
H - 12. OILSILK	L. General Macarthur's cause of death
S - 13. BEACH	M. Drowned when allowed to swim too far out to sea
C - 14. WARGRAVE	N. Abandoned a group of men under attack
U - 15. REVOLVER	O. Emily noticed one on the dining room window.
G - 16. COMBES	P. Armstrong was missing this item from his bag.
Y - 17. DAVIS	Q. Had an affair with his friend's wife
B - 18. INDIAN	R. Vera's last name
L - 19. BLUDGEONING	S. Where Armstrong's body was found
O - 20. BEE	T. Killed someone for sleeping with his wife
V - 21. CLOCK	U. Lombard brought this weapon to the island.
E - 22. SECRETARY	V. Blore was killed with this item.
D - 23. HANGING	W. Drowned herself after becoming pregnant
W - 24. BEATRICE	X. Mr. Lombard's first name
Q - 25. ARTHUR	Y. Mr. Blore's assumed name when he arrived on the island

And Then There Were None Matching 3

___ 1. MACARTHUR   A. Knew that murder had been committed to win his love
___ 2. HOOK   B. Allowed a weak young boy to drown
___ 3. YARN   C. Mr. Lombard's first name
___ 4. TONGUE   D. Vera's hired position with Mrs. Owen
___ 5. SWAN   E. Vera's last name
___ 6. MURDER   F. Ten of these figures were on the table in the beginning.
___ 7. SECRETARY   G. Had an affair with his friend's wife
___ 8. NURSERY   H. Died on the operating table
___ 9. CYRIL   I. Led someone to suicide through moral judgment
___10. BEAR   J. The voice accused each of the guests of this.
___11. PHILLIP   K. Wargrave was said to look like a wary old one of these.
___12. OILSILK   L. Killed an employer by withholding medicine
___13. MARSTON   M. This curtain was missing from the bathroom.
___14. BEE   N. Title of the song on the gramophone: ___ Song
___15. NARRACOTT   O. Captain of the boat that took the guests to the island
___16. CLEES   P. Blore was killed with this item.
___17. TORTOISE   Q. The group was reduced to eating this.
___18. CLOCK   R. Emily was missing it, and it turned up on the judge.
___19. INDIAN   S. Killed someone by being too reckless
___20. HUGO   T. Emily noticed one on the dining room window.
___21. EMILY   U. The marble clock was in this shape
___22. ARTHUR   V. Drowned when allowed to swim too far out to sea
___23. ROGERS   W. The murders followed the ___ rhyme.
___24. VERA   X. Vera noticed this in the ceiling near her bed.
___25. CLAYTHORNE   Y. Killed someone for sleeping with his wife

And Then There Were None Matching 3 Answer Key

Y - 1. MACARTHUR	A.	Knew that murder had been committed to win his love
X - 2. HOOK	B.	Allowed a weak young boy to drown
R - 3. YARN	C.	Mr. Lombard's first name
Q - 4. TONGUE	D.	Vera's hired position with Mrs. Owen
N - 5. SWAN	E.	Vera's last name
J - 6. MURDER	F.	Ten of these figures were on the table in the beginning.
D - 7. SECRETARY	G.	Had an affair with his friend's wife
W - 8. NURSERY	H.	Died on the operating table
V - 9. CYRIL	I.	Led someone to suicide through moral judgment
U - 10. BEAR	J.	The voice accused each of the guests of this.
C - 11. PHILLIP	K.	Wargrave was said to look like a wary old one of these.
M - 12. OILSILK	L.	Killed an employer by withholding medicine
S - 13. MARSTON	M.	This curtain was missing from the bathroom.
T - 14. BEE	N.	Title of the song on the gramophone: ___ Song
O - 15. NARRACOTT	O.	Captain of the boat that took the guests to the island
H - 16. CLEES	P.	Blore was killed with this item.
K - 17. TORTOISE	Q.	The group was reduced to eating this.
P - 18. CLOCK	R.	Emily was missing it, and it turned up on the judge.
F - 19. INDIAN	S.	Killed someone by being too reckless
A - 20. HUGO	T.	Emily noticed one on the dining room window.
I - 21. EMILY	U.	The marble clock was in this shape
G - 22. ARTHUR	V.	Drowned when allowed to swim too far out to sea
L - 23. ROGERS	W.	The murders followed the ___ rhyme.
B - 24. VERA	X.	Vera noticed this in the ceiling near her bed.
E - 25. CLAYTHORNE	Y.	Killed someone for sleeping with his wife

And Then There Were None Matching 4

___ 1. SECRETARY   A. Famous for making harsh judgments
___ 2. CYRIL   B. Vera's means of death
___ 3. DAVIS   C. Killed an employer by withholding medicine
___ 4. SYRINGE   D. Drowned when allowed to swim too far out to sea
___ 5. HANGING   E. The voice accused each of the guests of this.
___ 6. BEACH   F. Killed someone for sleeping with his wife
___ 7. MURDER   G. Armstrong was missing this item from his bag.
___ 8. OWEN   H. Beatrice's last name
___ 9. ENGLAND   I. The guests anxiously awaited its arrival, but it never came.
___10. REVOLVER   J. Title of the song on the gramophone: ___ Song
___11. BOAT   K. Captain of the boat that took the guests to the island
___12. SWAN   L. Marston's cause of death
___13. BOTTLE   M. A fisherman found the confession in this.
___14. NARRACOTT   N. Abandoned a group of men under attack
___15. VERA   O. Supposed owner of the island: Mr. U. N. ___
___16. TAYLOR   P. Killed someone by being too reckless
___17. ROGERS   Q. Lombard brought this weapon to the island.
___18. LOMBARD   R. Job of Mr. Rogers
___19. INDIAN   S. Ten of these figures were on the table in the beginning.
___20. MARSTON   T. Vera's hired position with Mrs. Owen
___21. WARGRAVE   U. Allowed a weak young boy to drown
___22. HOOK   V. Where Armstrong's body was found
___23. POISON   W. Vera noticed this in the ceiling near her bed.
___24. BUTLER   X. Mr. Blore's assumed name when he arrived on the island
___25. MACARTHUR   Y. Country in which the story takes place

And Then There Were None Matching 4 Answer Key

T - 1. SECRETARY	A.	Famous for making harsh judgments
D - 2. CYRIL	B.	Vera's means of death
X - 3. DAVIS	C.	Killed an employer by withholding medicine
G - 4. SYRINGE	D.	Drowned when allowed to swim too far out to sea
B - 5. HANGING	E.	The voice accused each of the guests of this.
V - 6. BEACH	F.	Killed someone for sleeping with his wife
E - 7. MURDER	G.	Armstrong was missing this item from his bag.
O - 8. OWEN	H.	Beatrice's last name
Y - 9. ENGLAND	I.	The guests anxiously awaited its arrival, but it never came.
Q -10. REVOLVER	J.	Title of the song on the gramophone: ___ Song
I - 11. BOAT	K.	Captain of the boat that took the guests to the island
J - 12. SWAN	L.	Marston's cause of death
M -13. BOTTLE	M.	A fisherman found the confession in this.
K -14. NARRACOTT	N.	Abandoned a group of men under attack
U -15. VERA	O.	Supposed owner of the island: Mr. U. N. ___
H -16. TAYLOR	P.	Killed someone by being too reckless
C -17. ROGERS	Q.	Lombard brought this weapon to the island.
N -18. LOMBARD	R.	Job of Mr. Rogers
S -19. INDIAN	S.	Ten of these figures were on the table in the beginning.
P -20. MARSTON	T.	Vera's hired position with Mrs. Owen
A -21. WARGRAVE	U.	Allowed a weak young boy to drown
W -22. HOOK	V.	Where Armstrong's body was found
L -23. POISON	W.	Vera noticed this in the ceiling near her bed.
R -24. BUTLER	X.	Mr. Blore's assumed name when he arrived on the island
F -25. MACARTHUR	Y.	Country in which the story takes place

And Then There Were None Magic Squares 1

Match the definition with the vocabulary word. Put your answers in the magic squares below. When your answers are correct, all columns and rows will add to the same number.

A. POE
B. POISON
C. BEE
D. TONGUE
E. LOMBARD
F. ARTHUR
G. MACARTHUR
H. INDIAN
I. MORRIS
J. DAVIS
K. PHILLIP
L. ROGERS
M. HERRING
N. SETON
O. HUGO
P. BLORE

1. Ten of these figures were on the table in the beginning.
2. False clue in a murder mystery: a red ___
3. Marston's cause of death
4. Mr. Lombard's first name
5. Mr. Blore's assumed name when he arrived on the island
6. Emily noticed one on the dining room window.
7. Committed perjury which led to the death of an innocent man
8. Abandoned a group of men under attack
9. Knew that murder had been committed to win his love
10. Had an affair with his friend's wife
11. Conducted the purchase of Indian Island for an unnamed third party
12. The group was reduced to eating this.
13. Credited as inventor of murder mystery genre
14. Killed an employer by withholding medicine
15. Killed someone for sleeping with his wife
16. Wargrave cooked HIS goose.

A=	B=	C=	D=
E=	F=	G=	H=
I=	J=	K=	L=
M=	N=	O=	P=

And Then There Were None Magic Squares 1 Answer Key

Match the definition with the vocabulary word. Put your answers in the magic squares below. When your answers are correct, all columns and rows will add to the same number.

A. POE
B. POISON
C. BEE
D. TONGUE
E. LOMBARD
F. ARTHUR
G. MACARTHUR
H. INDIAN
I. MORRIS
J. DAVIS
K. PHILLIP
L. ROGERS
M. HERRING
N. SETON
O. HUGO
P. BLORE

1. Ten of these figures were on the table in the beginning.
2. False clue in a murder mystery: a red ___
3. Marston's cause of death
4. Mr. Lombard's first name
5. Mr. Blore's assumed name when he arrived on the island
6. Emily noticed one on the dining room window.
7. Committed perjury which led to the death of an innocent man
8. Abandoned a group of men under attack
9. Knew that murder had been committed to win his love
10. Had an affair with his friend's wife
11. Conducted the purchase of Indian Island for an unnamed third party
12. The group was reduced to eating this.
13. Credited as inventor of murder mystery genre
14. Killed an employer by withholding medicine
15. Killed someone for sleeping with his wife
16. Wargrave cooked HIS goose.

A=13	B=3	C=6	D=12
E=8	F=10	G=15	H=1
I=11	J=5	K=4	L=14
M=2	N=16	O=9	P=7

Copyrighted

And Then There Were None Magic Squares 2

Match the definition with the vocabulary word. Put your answers in the magic squares below. When your answers are correct, all columns and rows will add to the same number.

A. TAYLOR
B. CHRISTIE
C. INDIAN
D. ISLAND
E. HUGO
F. MACARTHUR
G. PHILLIP
H. BEACH
I. CYRIL
J. OILSILK
K. BLUDGEONING
L. BOAT
M. POE
N. KNITTING
O. ARTHUR
P. CLOCK

1. Killed someone for sleeping with his wife
2. Drowned when allowed to swim too far out to sea
3. Had an affair with his friend's wife
4. Setting of the novel: Indian ___
5. Credited as inventor of murder mystery genre
6. Author of And Then There Were None
7. Where Armstrong's body was found
8. General Macarthur's cause of death
9. Ten of these figures were on the table in the beginning.
10. Blore was killed with this item.
11. This curtain was missing from the bathroom.
12. Knew that murder had been committed to win his love
13. The guests anxiously awaited its arrival, but it never came.
14. Mr. Lombard's first name
15. Beatrice's last name
16. Emily's pastime

A=	B=	C=	D=
E=	F=	G=	H=
I=	J=	K=	L=
M=	N=	O=	P=

And Then There Were None Magic Squares 2 Answer Key

Match the definition with the vocabulary word. Put your answers in the magic squares below. When your answers are correct, all columns and rows will add to the same number.

A. TAYLOR
B. CHRISTIE
C. INDIAN
D. ISLAND
E. HUGO
F. MACARTHUR
G. PHILLIP
H. BEACH
I. CYRIL
J. OILSILK
K. BLUDGEONING
L. BOAT
M. POE
N. KNITTING
O. ARTHUR
P. CLOCK

1. Killed someone for sleeping with his wife
2. Drowned when allowed to swim too far out to sea
3. Had an affair with his friend's wife
4. Setting of the novel: Indian ___
5. Credited as inventor of murder mystery genre
6. Author of And Then There Were None
7. Where Armstrong's body was found
8. General Macarthur's cause of death
9. Ten of these figures were on the table in the beginning.
10. Blore was killed with this item.
11. This curtain was missing from the bathroom.
12. Knew that murder had been committed to win his love
13. The guests anxiously awaited its arrival, but it never came.
14. Mr. Lombard's first name
15. Beatrice's last name
16. Emily's pastime

A=15	B=6	C=9	D=4
E=12	F=1	G=14	H=7
I=2	J=11	K=8	L=13
M=5	N=16	O=3	P=10

And Then There Were None Magic Squares 3

Match the definition with the vocabulary word. Put your answers in the magic squares below. When your answers are correct, all columns and rows will add to the same number.

A. WARGRAVE
B. DAVIS
C. INDIAN
D. ARTHUR
E. BOTTLE
F. BUTLER
G. MORRIS
H. LOMBARD
I. REVOLVER
J. HANGING
K. ISLAND
L. HOOK
M. BLORE
N. CHRISTIE
O. SWAN
P. YARN

1. Ten of these figures were on the table in the beginning.
2. Vera's means of death
3. Job of Mr. Rogers
4. Title of the song on the gramophone: ___ Song
5. Emily was missing it, and it turned up on the judge.
6. A fisherman found the confession in this.
7. Lombard brought this weapon to the island.
8. Had an affair with his friend's wife
9. Committed perjury which led to the death of an innocent man
10. Abandoned a group of men under attack
11. Vera noticed this in the ceiling near her bed.
12. Famous for making harsh judgments
13. Mr. Blore's assumed name when he arrived on the island
14. Setting of the novel: Indian ___
15. Conducted the purchase of Indian Island for an unnamed third party
16. Author of And Then There Were None

A=	B=	C=	D=
E=	F=	G=	H=
I=	J=	K=	L=
M=	N=	O=	P=

And Then There Were None Magic Squares 3 Answer Key

Match the definition with the vocabulary word. Put your answers in the magic squares below. When your answers are correct, all columns and rows will add to the same number.

A. WARGRAVE
B. DAVIS
C. INDIAN
D. ARTHUR
E. BOTTLE
F. BUTLER
G. MORRIS
H. LOMBARD
I. REVOLVER
J. HANGING
K. ISLAND
L. HOOK
M. BLORE
N. CHRISTIE
O. SWAN
P. YARN

1. Ten of these figures were on the table in the beginning.
2. Vera's means of death
3. Job of Mr. Rogers
4. Title of the song on the gramophone: ___ Song
5. Emily was missing it, and it turned up on the judge.
6. A fisherman found the confession in this.
7. Lombard brought this weapon to the island.
8. Had an affair with his friend's wife
9. Committed perjury which led to the death of an innocent man
10. Abandoned a group of men under attack
11. Vera noticed this in the ceiling near her bed.
12. Famous for making harsh judgments
13. Mr. Blore's assumed name when he arrived on the island
14. Setting of the novel: Indian ___
15. Conducted the purchase of Indian Island for an unnamed third party
16. Author of And Then There Were None

A=12	B=13	C=1	D=8
E=6	F=3	G=15	H=10
I=7	J=2	K=14	L=11
M=9	N=16	O=4	P=5

And Then There Were None Magic Squares 4

Match the definition with the vocabulary word. Put your answers in the magic squares below. When your answers are correct, all columns and rows will add to the same number.

A. ARTHUR
B. COMBES
C. ISLAND
D. OILSILK
E. BEAR
F. ENGLAND
G. POISON
H. TAYLOR
I. VERA
J. REVOLVER
K. BRADY
L. BEE
M. AXE
N. DAVIS
O. MURDER
P. HANGING

1. The voice accused each of the guests of this.
2. This curtain was missing from the bathroom.
3. Lombard brought this weapon to the island.
4. The marble clock was in this shape
5. Allowed a weak young boy to drown
6. Country in which the story takes place
7. Vera's means of death
8. Setting of the novel: Indian ___
9. Beatrice's last name
10. Died after necessary medicine was withheld
11. Had an affair with his friend's wife
12. Mr. Blore's assumed name when he arrived on the island
13. Was run down by a reckless driver
14. Rogers was killed with this.
15. Marston's cause of death
16. Emily noticed one on the dining room window.

A=	B=	C=	D=
E=	F=	G=	H=
I=	J=	K=	L=
M=	N=	O=	P=

And Then There Were None Magic Squares 4 Answer Key

Match the definition with the vocabulary word. Put your answers in the magic squares below. When your answers are correct, all columns and rows will add to the same number.

A. ARTHUR
B. COMBES
C. ISLAND
D. OILSILK
E. BEAR
F. ENGLAND
G. POISON
H. TAYLOR
I. VERA
J. REVOLVER
K. BRADY
L. BEE
M. AXE
N. DAVIS
O. MURDER
P. HANGING

1. The voice accused each of the guests of this.
2. This curtain was missing from the bathroom.
3. Lombard brought this weapon to the island.
4. The marble clock was in this shape
5. Allowed a weak young boy to drown
6. Country in which the story takes place
7. Vera's means of death
8. Setting of the novel: Indian ___
9. Beatrice's last name
10. Died after necessary medicine was withheld
11. Had an affair with his friend's wife
12. Mr. Blore's assumed name when he arrived on the island
13. Was run down by a reckless driver
14. Rogers was killed with this.
15. Marston's cause of death
16. Emily noticed one on the dining room window.

A=11	B=13	C=8	D=2
E=4	F=6	G=15	H=9
I=5	J=3	K=10	L=16
M=14	N=12	O=1	P=7

And Then There Were None Word Search 1

A	R	T	H	U	R	U	H	T	R	A	C	A	M	N	N	L	K	L	B
I	G	N	I	R	R	E	H	G	A	Y	P	G	N	A	N	C	R	I	W
N	X	S	N	Q	G	P	G	N	R	Y	M	O	W	F	O	J	Y	T	V
D	M	J	Y	D	M	P	X	I	H	D	L	S	I	L	S	L	N	T	V
I	J	F	U	S	X	H	L	G	B	T	K	O	C	S	Y	V	K	L	P
A	L	J	R	R	B	Z	B	N	O	L	P	M	R	F	O	T	F	E	B
N	M	W	W	E	P	U	C	A	T	G	M	U	Q	Q	V	N	B	L	Q
N	C	O	S	G	P	F	T	H	T	W	C	R	W	B	P	C	O	N	S
U	D	M	R	O	D	X	S	L	L	V	B	D	E	S	O	R	M	K	T
R	T	W	A	R	G	R	A	V	E	O	W	E	N	S	E	E	L	C	R
S	S	B	H	F	I	L	F	R	P	R	C	R	A	X	U	M	V	D	V
E	D	E	U	B	K	S	A	W	M	I	Y	D	A	R	G	K	I	H	T
R	N	A	G	O	K	Y	J	Y	R	D	R	A	N	S	N	L	I	L	V
Y	S	C	O	M	B	E	S	T	B	A	T	O	R	T	O	I	S	E	Y
V	H	H	H	Q	Y	R	A	Y	B	V	C	K	A	N	T	S	L	R	X
D	N	A	L	G	N	E	A	M	M	I	M	O	W	Q	E	L	A	F	R
H	S	T	M	P	B	F	O	D	F	S	B	Z	K	P	S	I	N	F	J
S	N	P	H	I	L	L	I	P	Y	B	D	M	Q	Y	W	O	D	Q	S

A fisherman found the confession in this. (6)
Abandoned a group of men under attack (7)
Allowed a weak young boy to drown (4)
Beatrice's last name (6)
Blore was killed with this item. (5)
Committed perjury which led to the death of an innocent man (5)
Conducted the purchase of Indian Island for an unnamed third party (6)
Country in which the story takes place (7)
Credited as inventor of murder mystery genre (3)
Died after necessary medicine was withheld (5)
Died on the operating table (5)
Drowned herself after becoming pregnant (8)
Drowned when allowed to swim too far out to sea (5)
Emily noticed one on the dining room window. (3)
Emily was missing it, and it turned up on the judge. (4)
False clue in a murder mystery: a red ___ (7)
Famous for making harsh judgments (8)
Had an affair with his friend's wife (6)
Job of Mr. Rogers (6)
Killed an employer by withholding medicine (6)
Killed someone for sleeping with his wife (9)
Knew that murder had been committed to win his love (4)
Led someone to suicide through moral judgment (5)

Marston's cause of death (6)
Mr. Blore's assumed name when he arrived on the island (5)
Mr. Lombard's first name (7)
Original title: Ten ___ Indians (6)
Rogers was killed with this. (3)
Setting of the novel: Indian ___ (6)
Supposed owner of the island: Mr. U. N. ___ (4)
Ten of these figures were on the table in the beginning. (6)
The group was reduced to eating this. (6)
The guests anxiously awaited its arrival, but it never came. (4)
The marble clock was in this shape (4)
The murders followed the ___ rhyme. (7)
The voice accused each of the guests of this. (6)
This curtain was missing from the bathroom. (7)
Title of the song on the gramophone: ___ Song (4)
Vera noticed this in the ceiling near her bed. (4)
Vera's means of death (7)
Wargrave cooked HIS goose. (5)
Wargrave was said to look like a wary old one of these. (8)
Wargrave's occupation (5)
Was run down by a reckless driver (6)
Where Armstrong's body was found (5)

And Then There Were None Word Search 1 Answer Key

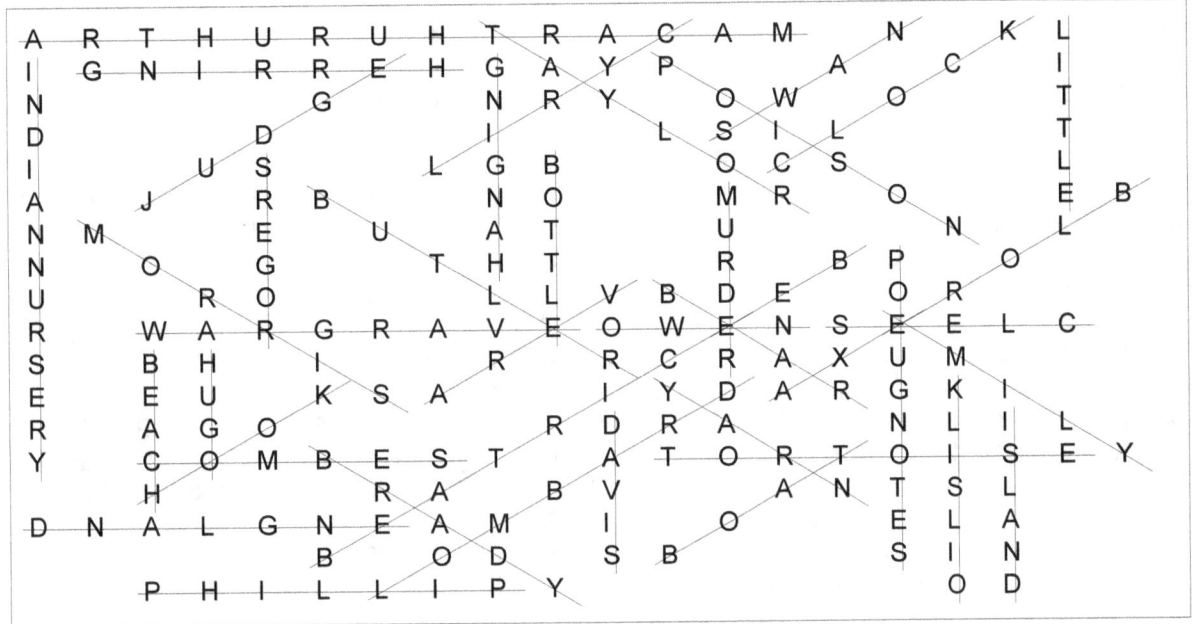

A fisherman found the confession in this. (6)
Abandoned a group of men under attack (7)
Allowed a weak young boy to drown (4)
Beatrice's last name (6)
Blore was killed with this item. (5)
Committed perjury which led to the death of an innocent man (5)
Conducted the purchase of Indian Island for an unnamed third party (6)
Country in which the story takes place (7)
Credited as inventor of murder mystery genre (3)
Died after necessary medicine was withheld (5)
Died on the operating table (5)
Drowned herself after becoming pregnant (8)
Drowned when allowed to swim too far out to sea (5)
Emily noticed one on the dining room window. (3)
Emily was missing it, and it turned up on the judge. (4)
False clue in a murder mystery: a red ___ (7)
Famous for making harsh judgments (8)
Had an affair with his friend's wife (6)
Job of Mr. Rogers (6)
Killed an employer by withholding medicine (6)
Killed someone for sleeping with his wife (9)
Knew that murder had been committed to win his love (4)
Led someone to suicide through moral judgment (5)

Marston's cause of death (6)
Mr. Blore's assumed name when he arrived on the island (5)
Mr. Lombard's first name (7)
Original title: Ten ___ Indians (6)
Rogers was killed with this. (3)
Setting of the novel: Indian ___ (6)
Supposed owner of the island: Mr. U. N. ___ (4)
Ten of these figures were on the table in the beginning. (6)
The group was reduced to eating this. (6)
The guests anxiously awaited its arrival, but it never came. (4)
The marble clock was in this shape (4)
The murders followed the ___ rhyme. (7)
The voice accused each of the guests of this. (6)
This curtain was missing from the bathroom. (7)
Title of the song on the gramophone: ___ Song (4)
Vera noticed this in the ceiling near her bed. (4)
Vera's means of death (7)
Wargrave cooked HIS goose. (5)
Wargrave was said to look like a wary old one of these. (8)
Wargrave's occupation (5)
Was run down by a reckless driver (6)
Where Armstrong's body was found (5)

And Then There Were None Word Search 2

```
M U R D E R P H I L L I P N F S H U G O
P L E V A R G R A W G V O E X E G D U J
C S L T N U R S E R Y T E W H C T L Y F
P K T A D N A L G N E I Z O H R T I H B
N G U Y M L W Y K S T H X Q Y E Z T C V
M A B L X N W D F S B O K L F T P T A H
K X R O B Z A A I S G N I G N A H L E B
R R S R E G O R A E B M B L O R E E B J
D R E T A T H B T L E A A X S Y W X H T
C N A V H C D M J H Q C S R J I L A Q N
T O D M O C O P O E U A W W S I L S G D
B S M N O L L T K X H R A F R T E K Z E
M I B B K C V O T K V T N Y V E O N G Y
K O S G E Y Z E C R B H C D L S A N A Q
X P R X L S A N R K W U C C Z I I R H Y
S R N R H E R R I N G R Y G D R E S C P
P D Y X I G W D N A L S I N Y V N Y Z J
Y Z D R R S T O N G U E I S I V A D K T
```

Allowed a weak young boy to drown (4)
Armstrong was missing this item from his bag. (7)
Author of And Then There Were None (8)
Beatrice's last name (6)
Blore was killed with this item. (5)
Captain of the boat that took the guests to the island (9)
Committed perjury which led to the death of an innocent man (5)
Conducted the purchase of Indian Island for an unnamed third party (6)
Country in which the story takes place (7)
Credited as inventor of murder mystery genre (3)
Died after necessary medicine was withheld (5)
Died on the operating table (5)
Drowned when allowed to swim too far out to sea (5)
Emily noticed one on the dining room window. (3)
Emily was missing it, and it turned up on the judge. (4)
Emily's last name (5)
False clue in a murder mystery: a red ___ (7)
Famous for making harsh judgments (8)
Had an affair with his friend's wife (6)
Job of Mr. Rogers (6)
Killed an employer by withholding medicine (6)
Killed someone by being too reckless (7)
Killed someone for sleeping with his wife (9)
Knew that murder had been committed to win his love (4)

Led someone to suicide through moral judgment (5)
Lombard brought this weapon to the island. (8)
Marston's cause of death (6)
Mr. Blore's assumed name when he arrived on the island (5)
Mr. Lombard's first name (7)
Original title: Ten ___ Indians (6)
Rogers was killed with this. (3)
Setting of the novel: Indian ___ (6)
Supposed owner of the island: Mr. U. N. ___ (4)
Ten of these figures were on the table in the beginning. (6)
The group was reduced to eating this. (6)
The guests anxiously awaited its arrival, but it never came. (4)
The marble clock was in this shape (4)
The murders followed the ___ rhyme. (7)
The voice accused each of the guests of this. (6)
This curtain was missing from the bathroom. (7)
Title of the song on the gramophone: ___ Song (4)
Vera noticed this in the ceiling near her bed. (4)
Vera's hired position with Mrs. Owen (9)
Vera's means of death (7)
Wargrave cooked HIS goose. (5)
Wargrave's occupation (5)
Was run down by a reckless driver (6)
Where Armstrong's body was found (5)

And Then There Were None Word Search 2 Answer Key

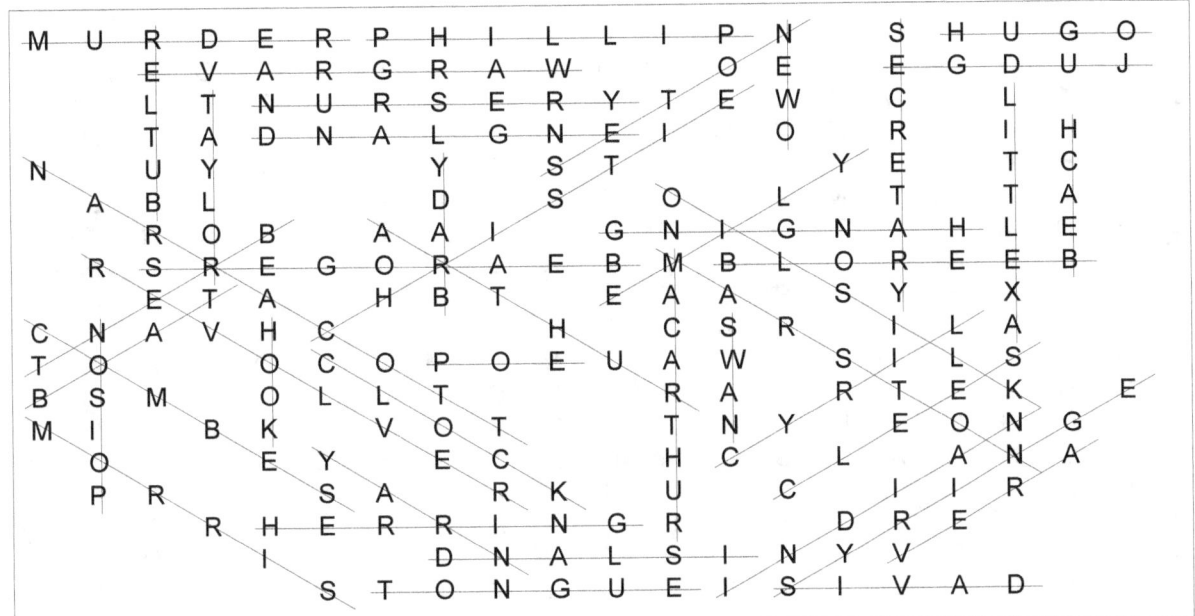

Allowed a weak young boy to drown (4)
Armstrong was missing this item from his bag. (7)
Author of And Then There Were None (8)
Beatrice's last name (6)
Blore was killed with this item. (5)
Captain of the boat that took the guests to the island (9)
Committed perjury which led to the death of an innocent man (5)
Conducted the purchase of Indian Island for an unnamed third party (6)
Country in which the story takes place (7)
Credited as inventor of murder mystery genre (3)
Died after necessary medicine was withheld (5)
Died on the operating table (5)
Drowned when allowed to swim too far out to sea (5)
Emily noticed one on the dining room window. (3)
Emily was missing it, and it turned up on the judge. (4)
Emily's last name (5)
False clue in a murder mystery: a red ___ (7)
Famous for making harsh judgments (8)
Had an affair with his friend's wife (6)
Job of Mr. Rogers (6)
Killed an employer by withholding medicine (6)
Killed someone by being too reckless (7)
Killed someone for sleeping with his wife (9)
Knew that murder had been committed to win his love (4)

Led someone to suicide through moral judgment (5)
Lombard brought this weapon to the island. (8)
Marston's cause of death (6)
Mr. Blore's assumed name when he arrived on the island (5)
Mr. Lombard's first name (7)
Original title: Ten ___ Indians (6)
Rogers was killed with this. (3)
Setting of the novel: Indian ___ (6)
Supposed owner of the island: Mr. U. N. ___ (4)
Ten of these figures were on the table in the beginning. (6)
The group was reduced to eating this. (6)
The guests anxiously awaited its arrival, but it never came. (4)
The marble clock was in this shape (4)
The murders followed the ___ rhyme. (7)
The voice accused each of the guests of this. (6)
This curtain was missing from the bathroom. (7)
Title of the song on the gramophone: ___ Song (4)
Vera noticed this in the ceiling near her bed. (4)
Vera's hired position with Mrs. Owen (9)
Vera's means of death (7)
Wargrave cooked HIS goose. (5)
Wargrave's occupation (5)
Was run down by a reckless driver (6)
Where Armstrong's body was found (5)

And Then There Were None Word Search 3

```
X B B H B C T J B E Z K H B B H M K S R
H H U G O G R S E B M O C R R B L O E E
C L T R G R H S S S Y L A E J T E R W
V H O N T K X C E R N E D N O L S G R
V E R A R E V H I R G E Y T T W G O Y
T A I O I N V L E M S I U A N E R L
Y S M S T G O Y R L B N Y D N K
L Y I D A T T U L R V Z A T D L D M
I R S A H C I P D E V I N N A N O J
M E V A N D A R E S E N B D A A V R
E N I N D U R R K O O V S N O S N K
O G D S G U U R H T L A I R L M O G
P E U G I M R N A U H T T R C A S L
C C J M N F S E V C R O J N S I N
C L L T G W T A C O M R Y L S O F
D O S E C R E T A R Y C T B K Q T P R
S C W A R G R A V E Y L A Y T H O R N
W K P H I L L I P C L A Y T H O R N E
```

ARTHUR	CHRISTIE	HOOK	MURDER	SETON
AXE	CLAYTHORNE	HUGO	NARRACOTT	SWAN
BEACH	CLEES	INDIAN	NURSERY	SYRINGE
BEAR	CLOCK	ISLAND	OILSILK	TAYLOR
BEE	COMBES	JUDGE	OWEN	TONGUE
BLORE	CYRIL	KNITTING	PHILLIP	TORTOISE
BOAT	DAVIS	LITTLE	POE	VERA
BOTTLE	EMILY	LOMBARD	POISON	WARGRAVE
BRADY	ENGLAND	MACARTHUR	REVOLVER	YARN
BRENT	HANGING	MARSTON	ROGERS	
BUTLER	HERRING	MORRIS	SECRETARY	

And Then There Were None Word Search 3 Answer Key

ARTHUR	CHRISTIE	HOOK	MURDER	SETON
AXE	CLAYTHORNE	HUGO	NARRACOTT	SWAN
BEACH	CLEES	INDIAN	NURSERY	SYRINGE
BEAR	CLOCK	ISLAND	OILSILK	TAYLOR
BEE	COMBES	JUDGE	OWEN	TONGUE
BLORE	CYRIL	KNITTING	PHILLIP	TORTOISE
BOAT	DAVIS	LITTLE	POE	VERA
BOTTLE	EMILY	LOMBARD	POISON	WARGRAVE
BRADY	ENGLAND	MACARTHUR	REVOLVER	YARN
BRENT	HANGING	MARSTON	ROGERS	
BUTLER	HERRING	MORRIS	SECRETARY	

And Then There Were None Word Search 4

```
K S E C R E T A R Y I S L A N D J R T K
N P F A E V O Z L D N E Y K M J U O A Y
I H E C D A N L R A D B C R P X D G Y K
T B T L R G B J R I M L N I G G E L L
T S K E U G U E B A O G U H N E R O Q
I E S E M R E N A N C C R Z I G S R B
N T W S L A F T R G C C K S N R H E E K
G O P O E W G T A O L H Y E O R O C M S
D N G B Q N Q I Y I G A F R S E O C I Q
R M O X I N D L T L N N N Y I H K H L F
S A D G P A Y G P S M V H D O L E R Y V
T C N C B R H R I I M O N P P C P I L H
K A K L F R V Z L L S V R V I Y C S G Y
H R T O T A H N L K C E D R B O T T L E
X T C C N C N K I F W R T A I S W I S N
A H P K E O R U H T R A F V V S M E A Z
X U H C R T N G P R E L T U B I E W N P
E R O L B T L O M B A R D Z N B S Z W H
```

ARTHUR	BRENT	HANGING	MACARTHUR	ROGERS
AXE	BUTLER	HERRING	MORRIS	SECRETARY
BEACH	CHRISTIE	HOOK	MURDER	SETON
BEAR	CLEES	HUGO	NARRACOTT	SWAN
BEATRICE	CLOCK	INDIAN	NURSERY	SYRINGE
BEE	COMBES	ISLAND	OILSILK	TAYLOR
BLORE	CYRIL	JUDGE	OWEN	TONGUE
BOAT	DAVIS	KNITTING	PHILLIP	VERA
BOTTLE	EMILY	LITTLE	POE	WARGRAVE
BRADY	ENGLAND	LOMBARD	POISON	YARN

And Then There Were None Word Search 4 Answer Key

ARTHUR	BRENT	HANGING	MACARTHUR	ROGERS
AXE	BUTLER	HERRING	MORRIS	SECRETARY
BEACH	CHRISTIE	HOOK	MURDER	SETON
BEAR	CLEES	HUGO	NARRACOTT	SWAN
BEATRICE	CLOCK	INDIAN	NURSERY	SYRINGE
BEE	COMBES	ISLAND	OILSILK	TAYLOR
BLORE	CYRIL	JUDGE	OWEN	TONGUE
BOAT	DAVIS	KNITTING	PHILLIP	VERA
BOTTLE	EMILY	LITTLE	POE	WARGRAVE
BRADY	ENGLAND	LOMBARD	POISON	YARN

And Then There Were None Crossword 1

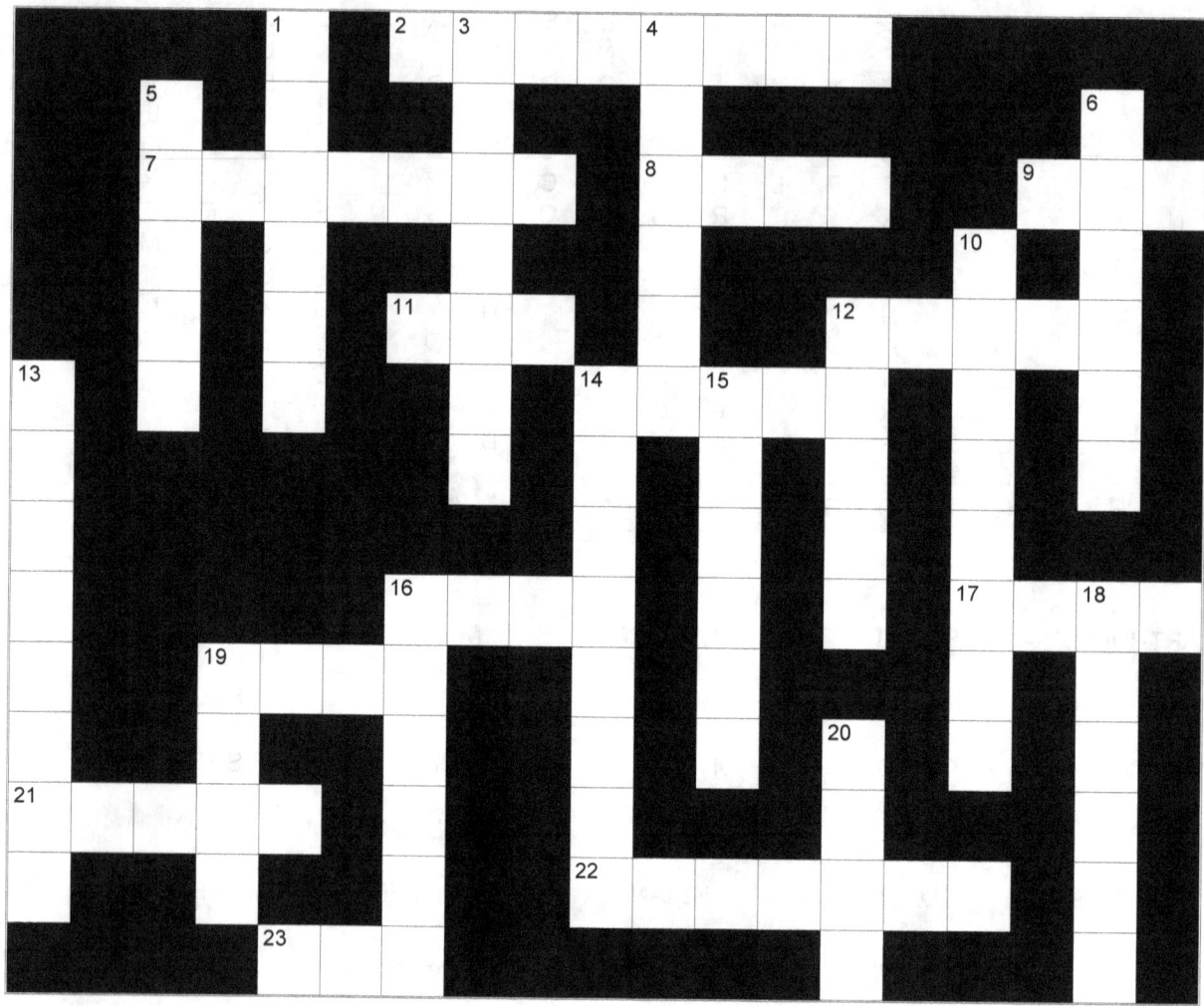

Across
2. Emily's pastime
7. Abandoned a group of men under attack
8. Emily was missing it, and it turned up on the judge.
9. Credited as inventor of murder mystery genre
11. Emily noticed one on the dining room window.
12. Died on the operating table
14. Died after necessary medicine was withheld
16. The guests anxiously awaited its arrival, but it never came.
17. Allowed a weak young boy to drown
19. Knew that murder had been committed to win his love
21. Wargrave cooked HIS goose.
22. Country in which the story takes place
23. Rogers was killed with this.

Down
1. Was run down by a reckless driver
3. The murders followed the ___ rhyme.
4. Beatrice's last name
5. Blore was killed with this item.
6. Marston's cause of death
10. Lombard brought this weapon to the island.
12. Drowned when allowed to swim too far out to sea
13. Wargrave was said to look like a wary old one of these.
14. Drowned herself after becoming pregnant
15. Had an affair with his friend's wife
16. A fisherman found the confession in this.
18. Killed an employer by withholding medicine
19. Vera noticed this in the ceiling near her bed.
20. Title of the song on the gramophone: ___ Song

And Then There Were None Crossword 1 Answer Key

Across
2. Emily's pastime
7. Abandoned a group of men under attack
8. Emily was missing it, and it turned up on the judge.
9. Credited as inventor of murder mystery genre
11. Emily noticed one on the dining room window.
12. Died on the operating table
14. Died after necessary medicine was withheld
16. The guests anxiously awaited its arrival, but it never came.
17. Allowed a weak young boy to drown
19. Knew that murder had been committed to win his love
21. Wargrave cooked HIS goose.
22. Country in which the story takes place
23. Rogers was killed with this.

Down
1. Was run down by a reckless driver
3. The murders followed the ___ rhyme.
4. Beatrice's last name
5. Blore was killed with this item.
6. Marston's cause of death
10. Lombard brought this weapon to the island.
12. Drowned when allowed to swim too far out to sea
13. Wargrave was said to look like a wary old one of these.
14. Drowned herself after becoming pregnant
15. Had an affair with his friend's wife
16. A fisherman found the confession in this.
18. Killed an employer by withholding medicine
19. Vera noticed this in the ceiling near her bed.
20. Title of the song on the gramophone: ___ Song

And Then There Were None Crossword 2

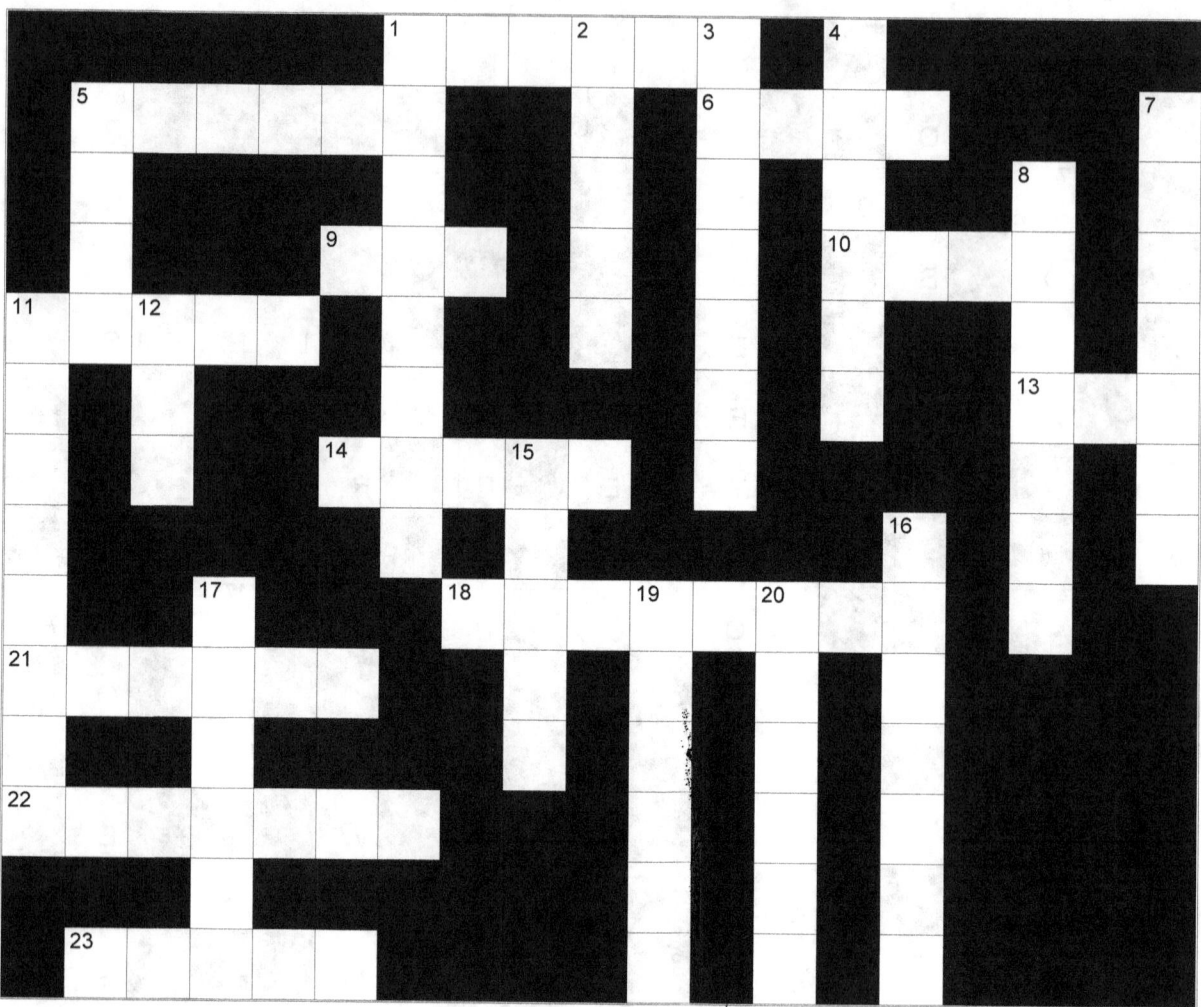

Across
1. Killed an employer by withholding medicine
5. A fisherman found the confession in this.
6. Emily was missing it, and it turned up on the judge.
9. Credited as inventor of murder mystery genre
10. Knew that murder had been committed to win his love
11. Died after necessary medicine was withheld
13. Emily noticed one on the dining room window.
14. Where Armstrong's body was found
18. Wargrave was said to look like a wary old one of these.
21. Setting of the novel: Indian ___
22. Country in which the story takes place
23. Drowned when allowed to swim too far out to sea

Down
1. Lombard brought this weapon to the island.
2. Led someone to suicide through moral judgment
3. Armstrong was missing this item from his bag.
4. Had an affair with his friend's wife
5. The marble clock was in this shape
7. The murders followed the ___ rhyme.
8. Abandoned a group of men under attack
11. Drowned herself after becoming pregnant
12. Rogers was killed with this.
15. Blore was killed with this item.
16. False clue in a murder mystery: a red ___
17. Beatrice's last name
19. The group was reduced to eating this.
20. Ten of these figures were on the table in the beginning.

And Then There Were None Crossword 2 Answer Key

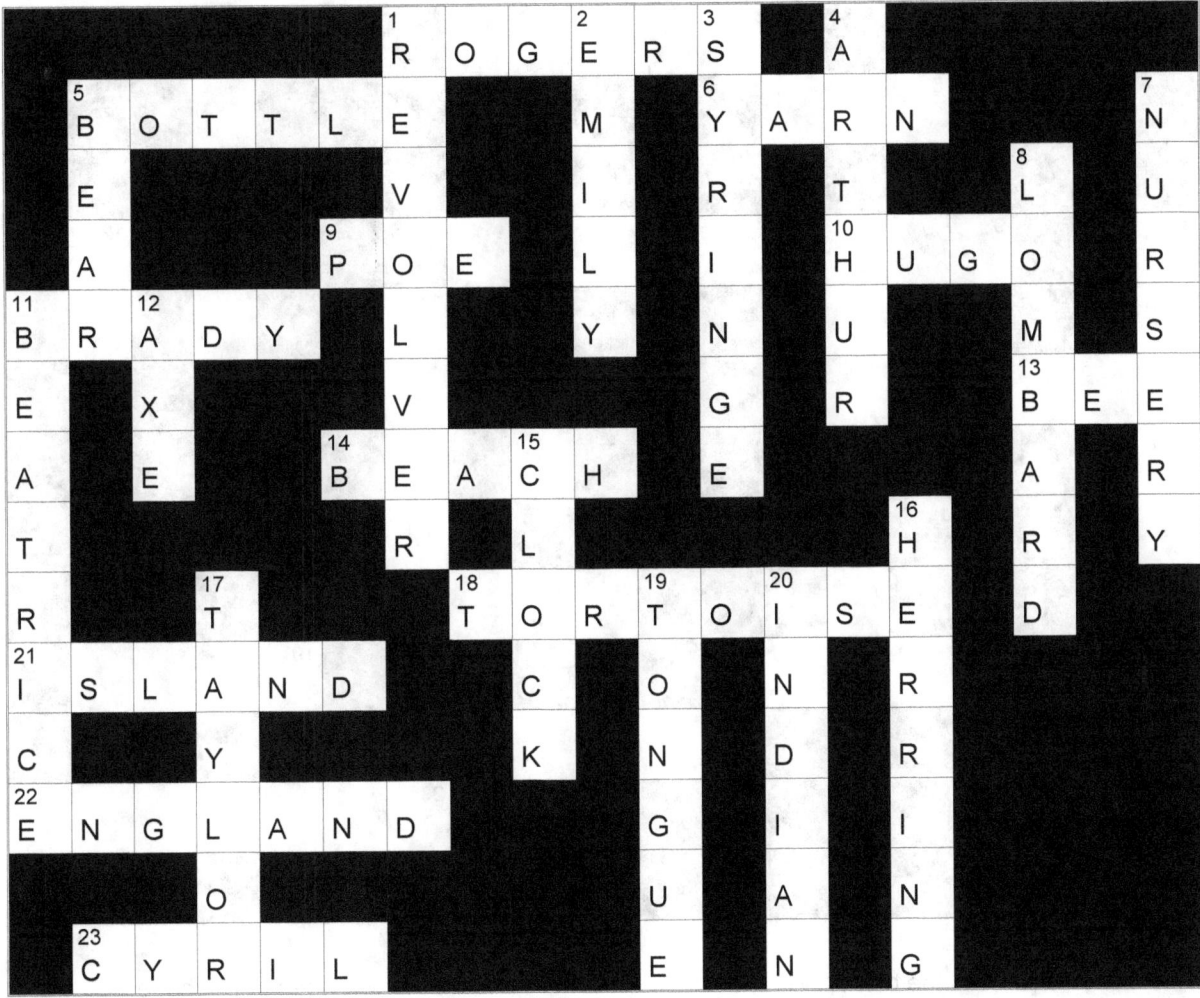

Across
1. Killed an employer by withholding medicine
5. A fisherman found the confession in this.
6. Emily was missing it, and it turned up on the judge.
9. Credited as inventor of murder mystery genre
10. Knew that murder had been committed to win his love
11. Died after necessary medicine was withheld
13. Emily noticed one on the dining room window.
14. Where Armstrong's body was found
18. Wargrave was said to look like a wary old one of these.
21. Setting of the novel: Indian ___
22. Country in which the story takes place
23. Drowned when allowed to swim too far out to sea

Down
1. Lombard brought this weapon to the island.
2. Led someone to suicide through moral judgment
3. Armstrong was missing this item from his bag.
4. Had an affair with his friend's wife
5. The marble clock was in this shape
7. The murders followed the ___ rhyme.
8. Abandoned a group of men under attack
11. Drowned herself after becoming pregnant
12. Rogers was killed with this.
15. Blore was killed with this item.
16. False clue in a murder mystery: a red ___
17. Beatrice's last name
19. The group was reduced to eating this.
20. Ten of these figures were on the table in the beginning.

And Then There Were None Crossword 3

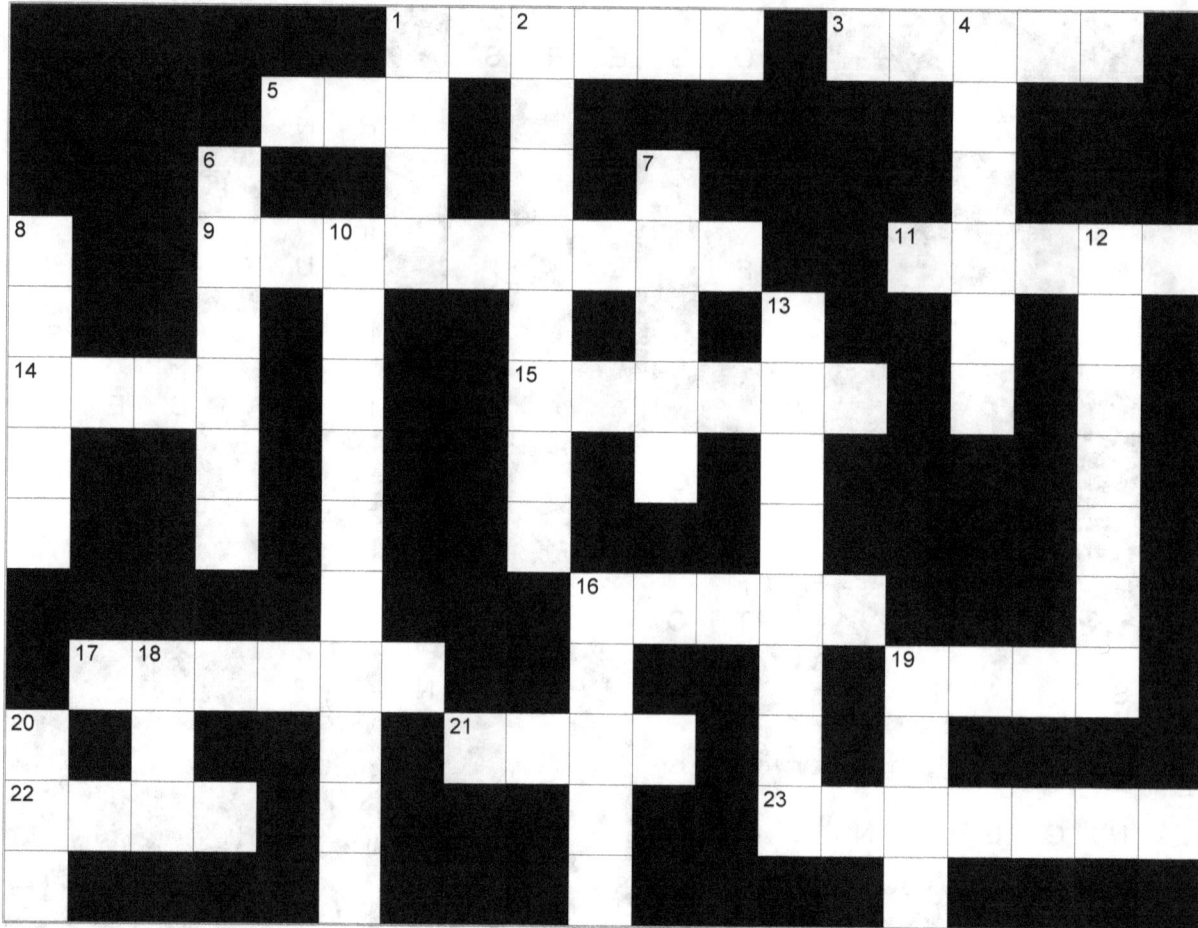

Across
1. A fisherman found the confession in this.
3. Drowned when allowed to swim too far out to sea
5. Emily noticed one on the dining room window.
9. Vera's hired position with Mrs. Owen
11. Wargrave cooked HIS goose.
14. Allowed a weak young boy to drown
15. Ten of these figures were on the table in the beginning.
16. Committed perjury which led to the death of an innocent man
17. Beatrice's last name
19. Vera noticed this in the ceiling near her bed.
21. Title of the song on the gramophone: ___ Song
22. Supposed owner of the island: Mr. U. N. ___
23. Country in which the story takes place

Down
1. The marble clock was in this shape
2. Wargrave was said to look like a wary old one of these.
4. Killed an employer by withholding medicine
6. Setting of the novel: Indian ___
7. Died after necessary medicine was withheld
8. Mr. Blore's assumed name when he arrived on the island
10. Vera's last name
12. This curtain was missing from the bathroom.
13. Famous for making harsh judgments
16. Where Armstrong's body was found
18. Rogers was killed with this.
19. Knew that murder had been committed to win his love
20. Credited as inventor of murder mystery genre

And Then There Were None Crossword 3 Answer Key

Across
1. A fisherman found the confession in this.
3. Drowned when allowed to swim too far out to sea
5. Emily noticed one on the dining room window.
9. Vera's hired position with Mrs. Owen
11. Wargrave cooked HIS goose.
14. Allowed a weak young boy to drown
15. Ten of these figures were on the table in the beginning.
16. Committed perjury which led to the death of an innocent man
17. Beatrice's last name
19. Vera noticed this in the ceiling near her bed.
21. Title of the song on the gramophone: ___ Song
22. Supposed owner of the island: Mr. U. N. ___
23. Country in which the story takes place

Down
1. The marble clock was in this shape
2. Wargrave was said to look like a wary old one of these.
4. Killed an employer by withholding medicine
6. Setting of the novel: Indian ___
7. Died after necessary medicine was withheld
8. Mr. Blore's assumed name when he arrived on the island
10. Vera's last name
12. This curtain was missing from the bathroom.
13. Famous for making harsh judgments
16. Where Armstrong's body was found
18. Rogers was killed with this.
19. Knew that murder had been committed to win his love
20. Credited as inventor of murder mystery genre

And Then There Were None Crossword 4

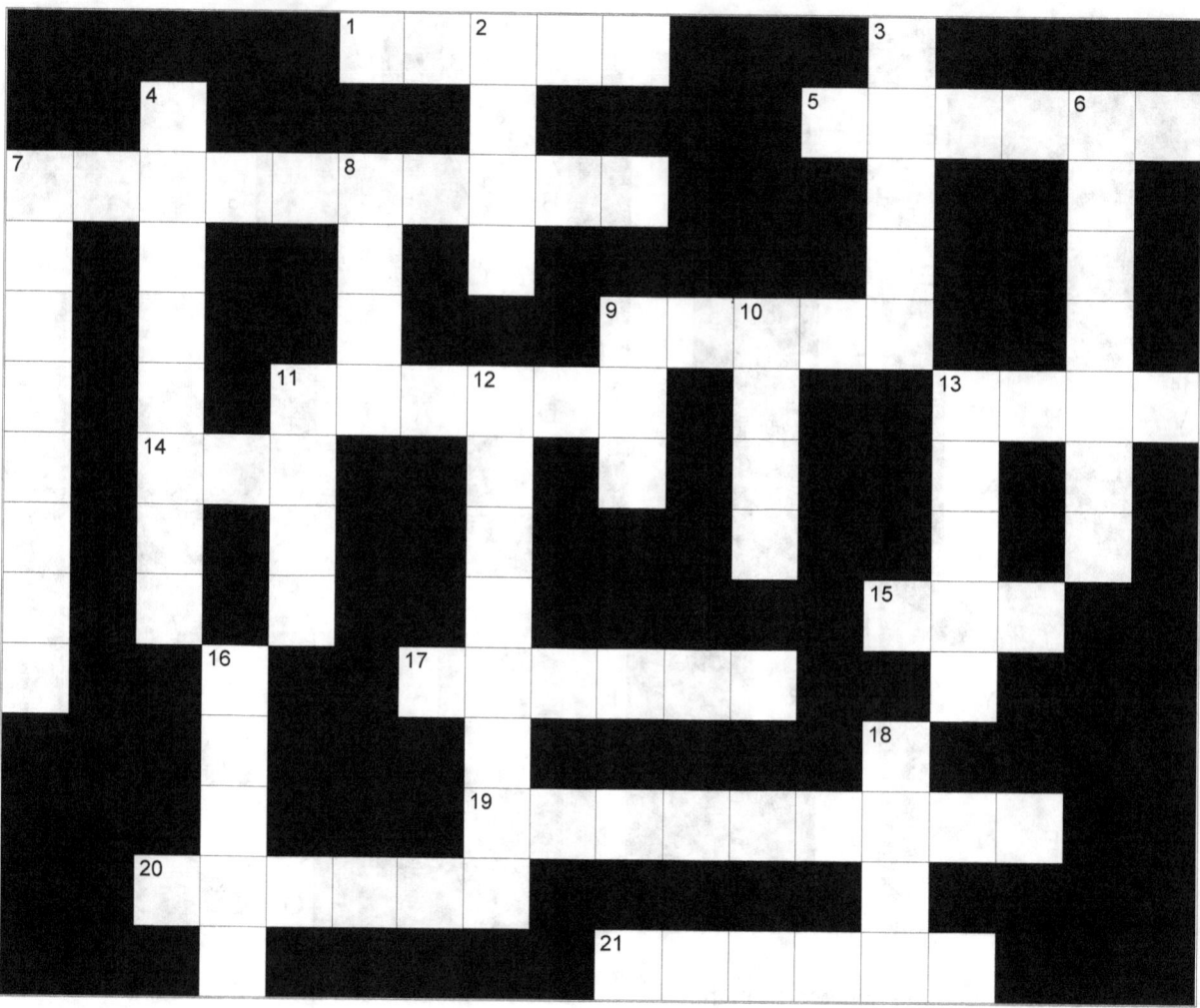

Across
1. Mr. Blore's assumed name when he arrived on the island
5. The voice accused each of the guests of this.
7. Vera's last name
9. Committed perjury which led to the death of an innocent man
11. A fisherman found the confession in this.
13. Title of the song on the gramophone: ___ Song
14. Rogers was killed with this.
15. Credited as inventor of murder mystery genre
17. Was run down by a reckless driver
19. Vera's hired position with Mrs. Owen
20. Original title: Ten ___ Indians
21. Setting of the novel: Indian ___

Down
2. Allowed a weak young boy to drown
3. Wargrave's occupation
4. Famous for making harsh judgments
6. Country in which the story takes place
7. Author of And Then There Were None
8. Knew that murder had been committed to win his love
9. Emily noticed one on the dining room window.
10. Supposed owner of the island: Mr. U. N. ___
11. The marble clock was in this shape
12. Wargrave was said to look like a wary old one of these.
13. Wargrave cooked HIS goose.
16. Drowned when allowed to swim too far out to sea
18. Emily was missing it, and it turned up on the judge.

And Then There Were None Crossword 4 Answer Key

Across
1. Mr. Blore's assumed name when he arrived on the island
5. The voice accused each of the guests of this.
7. Vera's last name
9. Committed perjury which led to the death of an innocent man
11. A fisherman found the confession in this.
13. Title of the song on the gramophone: ___ Song
14. Rogers was killed with this.
15. Credited as inventor of murder mystery genre
17. Was run down by a reckless driver
19. Vera's hired position with Mrs. Owen
20. Original title: Ten ___ Indians
21. Setting of the novel: Indian ___

Down
2. Allowed a weak young boy to drown
3. Wargrave's occupation
4. Famous for making harsh judgments
6. Country in which the story takes place
7. Author of And Then There Were None
8. Knew that murder had been committed to win his love
9. Emily noticed one on the dining room window.
10. Supposed owner of the island: Mr. U. N. ___
11. The marble clock was in this shape
12. Wargrave was said to look like a wary old one of these.
13. Wargrave cooked HIS goose.
16. Drowned when allowed to swim too far out to sea
18. Emily was missing it, and it turned up on the judge.

And Then There Were None

CHRISTIE	ROGERS	TORTOISE	WARGRAVE	MACARTHUR
LOMBARD	BOAT	POE	CLAYTHORNE	INDIAN
BLORE	BRADY	FREE SPACE	NARRACOTT	OILSILK
CYRIL	HERRING	EMILY	BEAR	NURSERY
ISLAND	BEATRICE	JUDGE	ENGLAND	OWEN

And Then There Were None

TONGUE	SWAN	BEE	LITTLE	AXE
SETON	SECRETARY	TAYLOR	YARN	PHILLIP
CLOCK	DAVIS	FREE SPACE	MORRIS	BLUDGEONING
CLEES	BUTLER	VERA	HUGO	HANGING
COMBES	BOTTLE	POISON	ARTHUR	KNITTING

And Then There Were None

AXE	SYRINGE	BUTLER	ENGLAND	POE
TONGUE	BEE	CLOCK	ROGERS	MACARTHUR
POISON	BEACH	FREE SPACE	NURSERY	PHILLIP
HANGING	BOTTLE	ARTHUR	YARN	TAYLOR
CLAYTHORNE	SETON	HUGO	MORRIS	BLUDGEONING

And Then There Were None

DAVIS	REVOLVER	JUDGE	HOOK	BEATRICE
COMBES	LOMBARD	KNITTING	VERA	EMILY
CYRIL	SECRETARY	FREE SPACE	NARRACOTT	CLEES
MARSTON	ISLAND	LITTLE	BEAR	BOAT
CHRISTIE	OWEN	HERRING	SWAN	OILSILK

And Then There Were None

ISLAND	SYRINGE	BLORE	TAYLOR	SECRETARY
EMILY	BRADY	BLUDGEONING	HANGING	HUGO
KNITTING	PHILLIP	FREE SPACE	CYRIL	BUTLER
CLAYTHORNE	SWAN	NARRACOTT	BEE	POE
MORRIS	WARGRAVE	AXE	POISON	ARTHUR

And Then There Were None

CLOCK	ENGLAND	BOAT	MARSTON	TORTOISE
OWEN	OILSILK	JUDGE	LOMBARD	SETON
LITTLE	MURDER	FREE SPACE	MACARTHUR	INDIAN
DAVIS	VERA	BOTTLE	NURSERY	CHRISTIE
HERRING	TONGUE	HOOK	ROGERS	YARN

And Then There Were None

MURDER	SETON	BEAR	BOAT	NARRACOTT
MACARTHUR	BLORE	AXE	OILSILK	BOTTLE
KNITTING	SWAN	FREE SPACE	VERA	MARSTON
ENGLAND	ISLAND	BEACH	SECRETARY	WARGRAVE
JUDGE	HANGING	CHRISTIE	CLOCK	BEE

And Then There Were None

BEATRICE	REVOLVER	ARTHUR	NURSERY	BUTLER
INDIAN	HERRING	LOMBARD	YARN	CLEES
SYRINGE	HUGO	FREE SPACE	CLAYTHORNE	POE
MORRIS	PHILLIP	ROGERS	POISON	TAYLOR
BLUDGEONING	DAVIS	OWEN	COMBES	HOOK

And Then There Were None

CLOCK	CLAYTHORNE	ISLAND	BRADY	HERRING
SECRETARY	COMBES	ENGLAND	ROGERS	PHILLIP
MARSTON	NARRACOTT	FREE SPACE	AXE	BEE
CHRISTIE	TORTOISE	WARGRAVE	TONGUE	MURDER
BLUDGEONING	POISON	HANGING	LITTLE	SETON

And Then There Were None

KNITTING	NURSERY	MACARTHUR	BOAT	BUTLER
BEAR	OILSILK	HOOK	INDIAN	EMILY
ARTHUR	CLEES	FREE SPACE	CYRIL	MORRIS
BEACH	VERA	TAYLOR	POE	REVOLVER
OWEN	HUGO	SWAN	SYRINGE	DAVIS

And Then There Were None

ARTHUR	CLOCK	WARGRAVE	REVOLVER	BEACH
HOOK	TAYLOR	COMBES	ROGERS	SETON
BRADY	INDIAN	FREE SPACE	LITTLE	OILSILK
TONGUE	JUDGE	HUGO	BEATRICE	MURDER
SECRETARY	BOAT	YARN	NURSERY	BLUDGEONING

And Then There Were None

KNITTING	NARRACOTT	CLAYTHORNE	BUTLER	PHILLIP
ISLAND	MARSTON	VERA	TORTOISE	LOMBARD
EMILY	HANGING	FREE SPACE	HERRING	BLORE
POISON	MACARTHUR	BOTTLE	CYRIL	SYRINGE
OWEN	DAVIS	CHRISTIE	SWAN	ENGLAND

And Then There Were None

TONGUE	REVOLVER	BOAT	BOTTLE	MURDER
MACARTHUR	VERA	INDIAN	BLORE	CLEES
ARTHUR	DAVIS	FREE SPACE	ISLAND	EMILY
AXE	CLAYTHORNE	OWEN	SWAN	YARN
POE	PHILLIP	HERRING	OILSILK	BLUDGEONING

And Then There Were None

MARSTON	ENGLAND	SECRETARY	BUTLER	KNITTING
JUDGE	WARGRAVE	COMBES	HOOK	SETON
TORTOISE	ROGERS	FREE SPACE	CHRISTIE	CYRIL
CLOCK	MORRIS	HANGING	LITTLE	BEE
SYRINGE	NURSERY	BEAR	HUGO	POISON

And Then There Were None

LOMBARD	ISLAND	LITTLE	BOAT	BEACH
TAYLOR	BEE	VERA	BOTTLE	TONGUE
POISON	BLORE	FREE SPACE	CLOCK	SYRINGE
SWAN	BEATRICE	POE	EMILY	BRADY
MORRIS	ROGERS	BUTLER	NARRACOTT	CYRIL

And Then There Were None

OILSILK	MACARTHUR	AXE	HOOK	DAVIS
COMBES	KNITTING	ARTHUR	INDIAN	BLUDGEONING
TORTOISE	HERRING	FREE SPACE	REVOLVER	SETON
WARGRAVE	ENGLAND	PHILLIP	CHRISTIE	MARSTON
MURDER	YARN	SECRETARY	NURSERY	BEAR

And Then There Were None

REVOLVER	BUTLER	COMBES	BOTTLE	ROGERS
INDIAN	SETON	NARRACOTT	OWEN	OILSILK
LOMBARD	MORRIS	FREE SPACE	BEAR	CLOCK
SECRETARY	CHRISTIE	TORTOISE	BEACH	EMILY
BOAT	BLORE	CYRIL	ENGLAND	NURSERY

And Then There Were None

LITTLE	WARGRAVE	CLEES	KNITTING	ISLAND
HERRING	AXE	TONGUE	BLUDGEONING	JUDGE
MURDER	BEATRICE	FREE SPACE	VERA	YARN
TAYLOR	DAVIS	SWAN	MARSTON	BRADY
MACARTHUR	SYRINGE	POE	HANGING	HUGO

And Then There Were None

SETON	CLOCK	DAVIS	CYRIL	VERA
NARRACOTT	ARTHUR	TORTOISE	CHRISTIE	LITTLE
HANGING	JUDGE	FREE SPACE	SYRINGE	OILSILK
BEE	BEACH	BUTLER	BEATRICE	ISLAND
BLORE	BOAT	POISON	BLUDGEONING	OWEN

And Then There Were None

INDIAN	MARSTON	BEAR	HUGO	BRADY
ROGERS	EMILY	REVOLVER	MURDER	AXE
PHILLIP	TONGUE	FREE SPACE	POE	MORRIS
COMBES	WARGRAVE	CLAYTHORNE	YARN	SECRETARY
SWAN	BOTTLE	HOOK	LOMBARD	NURSERY

And Then There Were None

LITTLE	SYRINGE	LOMBARD	VERA	HOOK
MURDER	BOAT	BLORE	MARSTON	SECRETARY
HERRING	SETON	FREE SPACE	DAVIS	PHILLIP
ARTHUR	ISLAND	BOTTLE	BEATRICE	JUDGE
HUGO	BLUDGEONING	TORTOISE	CLAYTHORNE	CHRISTIE

And Then There Were None

BEACH	NARRACOTT	POISON	REVOLVER	TAYLOR
BRADY	BEAR	OILSILK	CLOCK	BUTLER
WARGRAVE	ENGLAND	FREE SPACE	KNITTING	ROGERS
CYRIL	CLEES	YARN	NURSERY	SWAN
MORRIS	MACARTHUR	POE	AXE	OWEN

And Then There Were None

YARN	SETON	BOAT	BLORE	JUDGE
EMILY	ARTHUR	CLEES	BUTLER	HOOK
WARGRAVE	NARRACOTT	FREE SPACE	LOMBARD	COMBES
BEACH	ISLAND	BRADY	AXE	SYRINGE
BEAR	SWAN	OILSILK	DAVIS	TONGUE

And Then There Were None

CHRISTIE	REVOLVER	OWEN	CLOCK	ROGERS
VERA	KNITTING	CYRIL	PHILLIP	CLAYTHORNE
LITTLE	MORRIS	FREE SPACE	MACARTHUR	POE
BEATRICE	BEE	HANGING	ENGLAND	NURSERY
TORTOISE	HERRING	TAYLOR	INDIAN	BLUDGEONING

And Then There Were None

CLEES	BRADY	ENGLAND	EMILY	BEE
MORRIS	TORTOISE	BOAT	MACARTHUR	BOTTLE
LOMBARD	MARSTON	FREE SPACE	BEATRICE	PHILLIP
SECRETARY	SWAN	NURSERY	KNITTING	YARN
REVOLVER	INDIAN	CYRIL	BLUDGEONING	SYRINGE

And Then There Were None

DAVIS	SETON	HANGING	BUTLER	BEAR
ISLAND	BLORE	OILSILK	LITTLE	HOOK
CHRISTIE	MURDER	FREE SPACE	TAYLOR	BEACH
POE	JUDGE	HUGO	TONGUE	OWEN
WARGRAVE	AXE	NARRACOTT	COMBES	CLOCK

And Then There Were None

MURDER	NARRACOTT	INDIAN	JUDGE	DAVIS
ROGERS	BUTLER	CYRIL	HANGING	POISON
YARN	BEATRICE	FREE SPACE	MARSTON	CHRISTIE
OILSILK	MACARTHUR	CLOCK	TAYLOR	WARGRAVE
TORTOISE	SYRINGE	OWEN	NURSERY	BEACH

And Then There Were None

MORRIS	BEAR	KNITTING	BLORE	VERA
HUGO	COMBES	PHILLIP	SWAN	POE
CLAYTHORNE	ISLAND	FREE SPACE	SETON	BEE
ARTHUR	AXE	EMILY	LITTLE	CLEES
HERRING	SECRETARY	TONGUE	BOTTLE	LOMBARD

And Then There Were None

ARTHUR	CLAYTHORNE	POISON	NURSERY	HANGING
HOOK	BUTLER	TAYLOR	SECRETARY	INDIAN
CHRISTIE	TORTOISE	FREE SPACE	MORRIS	SWAN
REVOLVER	BLORE	WARGRAVE	KNITTING	MURDER
EMILY	PHILLIP	CLEES	ISLAND	BRADY

And Then There Were None

CYRIL	COMBES	NARRACOTT	LOMBARD	CLOCK
BEE	JUDGE	OWEN	BEAR	YARN
MACARTHUR	LITTLE	FREE SPACE	POE	SYRINGE
HUGO	ENGLAND	BEATRICE	HERRING	ROGERS
OILSILK	VERA	BOTTLE	BOAT	DAVIS

And Then There Were None

HANGING	INDIAN	POE	WARGRAVE	LOMBARD
DAVIS	SETON	NURSERY	CLEES	BEAR
LITTLE	BOTTLE	FREE SPACE	CHRISTIE	ARTHUR
COMBES	PHILLIP	SECRETARY	OILSILK	CLOCK
NARRACOTT	TAYLOR	BLUDGEONING	EMILY	MARSTON

And Then There Were None

REVOLVER	BLORE	MORRIS	VERA	YARN
HOOK	ENGLAND	JUDGE	BUTLER	MURDER
BEE	SYRINGE	FREE SPACE	BRADY	SWAN
BEACH	HUGO	BEATRICE	MACARTHUR	CLAYTHORNE
CYRIL	OWEN	ISLAND	TONGUE	AXE

And Then There Were None Vocabulary Word List

No.	Word	Clue/Definition
1.	ABHORRENT	Detestable; loathsome; hateful
2.	ABSTRACT	Theoretical; not applied or practical
3.	ADMONITORY	Serving to warn, especially to correct
4.	ADROITNESS	Expertise or nimbleness in the use of the hands or body
5.	AEONS	Indefinitely long periods of time
6.	AFFABLY	In a friendly, cordial manner
7.	AMPOULE	Sealed glass or plastic bulb containing solutions for hypodermic injection
8.	ANGULARITIES	Sharp corners; angular outlines
9.	ASPHYXIATION	Death by choking, smothering, or suffocating
10.	AUTOMATON	Mechanical figure; robot
11.	BARRICADED	Blocked with a defensive barrier
12.	CAIRNGORM	Smoky-yellow to dark brown or black variety of quartz, used as a gem stone
13.	CHANCERY	Division of the High Court of Justice of Great Britain
14.	CLAMBERED	Climbed with difficulty, especially on all fours
15.	CONCLAVE	Private or secret meeting
16.	CONCURRED	Was of the same opinion; agreed
17.	CONJURING	Affecting or influencing as if by invocation or a magic spell
18.	COUNTENANCE	Look or expression of the face
19.	COVERTLY	Secretly; in a concealed manner
20.	CRYPTIC	Mysterious in meaning; puzzling; ambiguous
21.	DEFERENTIAL	Showing regard or respect
22.	DEPORTMENT	Demeanor; conduct; behavior
23.	DESULTORY	Lacking in consistency or visible order; disconnected
24.	DOGGEREL	Crudely or irregularly fashioned verse, often of a humorous or burlesque nature
25.	DRAUGHT	Dose of liquid medicine
26.	DUBIOUSLY	In a doubtful manner
27.	EBONITE	Hard, non-resilient rubber formed by vulcanizing natural rubber
28.	EJACULATIONS	Sudden, short exclamations, especially brief pious utterances or prayers
29.	EXIGENCIES	Pressing or urgent situations
30.	FEASIBLE	Capable of being done, effected, or accomplished
31.	GIDDINESS	Dizziness
32.	GIMLET	Small tool for boring holes
33.	HELIOGRAPHING	Transmitting messages by reflecting sunlight
34.	HITHERTO	Up to this time; until now
35.	IMPROMPTU	Made or done without previous preparation
36.	INCLINATION	Disposition or bent, esp. of the mind or will; a liking or preference
37.	INDICTMENTS	Written statements charging a party with the commission of a crime
38.	INERT	Unable to move or act
39.	INEVITABILITY	Unable to be avoided, evaded, or escaped
40.	INNOCUOUS	Harmless
41.	INQUEST	Investigation made by a coroner into the cause of a death
42.	INTERVAL	In between period of time
43.	JETTY	Wharf; landing pier
44.	LARDER	Room or place where food is stored; pantry
45.	LASSITUDE	Weariness of body or mind from strain; lack of energy

And Then There Were None Vocabulary Word List

No.	Word	Clue/Definition
46.	LEGACY	Gift of property or money through a will; a bequest
47.	MACKINTOSH	Raincoat
48.	MALEVOLENTLY	In an evil, harmful, or injurious manner
49.	MALICIOUS	Deliberately harmful or spiteful
50.	OBLIQUELY	Having a slanting or sloping direction, course, or position
51.	OBLIVION	State of being completely forgotten or unknown
52.	OILSILK	Heavy, water-resistant fabric
53.	PACIFICALLY	Peaceably, mildly, calmly, or quietly
54.	PALL	Anything that covers, shrouds, or overspreads, esp. with darkness or gloom
55.	PALPABLY	Plainly seen, heard, or perceived; obviously
56.	PERITONITIS	Inflammation of the membrane surrounding the abdominal cavity
57.	PETROL	Gasoline
58.	PHYSIQUE	Physical or bodily structure; appearance
59.	PIOUS	Characterized by a hypocritical concern with virtue or religious devotion
60.	PRETENCE	False showing
61.	PROBATIONER	Nurse in training who is undergoing a trial period
62.	PROVISIONED	Provided a stock of necessary supplies, especially food
63.	QUIETUS	Discharge or release from life
64.	RECOILED	Shrunk back, as in fear or repugnance
65.	RECONNAISSANCE	Search made for useful military information in the field
66.	RECRIMINATION	Act of accusing in return
67.	REPROACH	Find fault with; blame; censure
68.	RIND	Thick and firm outer coat or covering
69.	RUMINATING	Reflecting on over and over again; turning a matter over in the mind
70.	SAGACITY	Acuteness of mental discernment and soundness of judgment
71.	SERENELY	In a calm, peaceful, or tranquil manner
72.	SIDEBOARD	Piece of dining room furniture having drawers and shelves for linens and tableware
73.	SIPHON	Pipe or tube to draw off or convey liquid
74.	SKEINS	Lengths of thread or yarn wound in loose, long coils
75.	SOLICITUDE	Attitude expressing excessive attentiveness
76.	STAMINA	Physical or moral strength to resist or withstand illness, fatigue, or hardship; endurance
77.	STILETTO	A samll dagger with a slender, tapering blade
78.	STUPENDOUS	Causing amazement; astounding; marvelous
79.	SUBSEQUENT	Occurring or coming later or after
80.	SUFFUSED	Spread through or over, as with liquid, color, or light
81.	SUPERLATIVELY	Of the highest kind, quality, or order; surpassing all else or others
82.	TENACIOUS	Holding fast; characterized by keeping a firm hold
83.	UNHEEDED	Disregarded; ignored
84.	UNOBTRUSIVELY	In a manner that is not undesirably noticeable or blatant
85.	UNTENANTED	Unoccupied; not leased to or occupied by a tenant
86.	VENTURE	Undertaking involving uncertainty as to the outcome
87.	VERISIMILITUDE	Appearance or semblance of truth; likelihood; probability

And Then There Were None Vocabulary Fill In The Blanks 1

_____ 1. Appearance or semblance of truth; likelihood; probability

_____ 2. Theoretical; not applied or practical

_____ 3. Capable of being done, effected, or accomplished

_____ 4. Provided a stock of necessary supplies, especially food

_____ 5. Smoky-yellow to dark brown or black variety of quartz, used as a gem stone

_____ 6. A small dagger with a slender, tapering blade

_____ 7. Expertise or nimbleness in the use of the hands or body

_____ 8. Holding fast; characterized by keeping a firm hold

_____ 9. In a doubtful manner

_____ 10. Unable to be avoided, evaded, or escaped

_____ 11. Weariness of body or mind from strain; lack of energy

_____ 12. Up to this time; until now

_____ 13. Acuteness of mental discernment and soundness of judgment

_____ 14. Sharp corners; angular outlines

_____ 15. Room or place where food is stored; pantry

_____ 16. Lengths of thread or yarn wound in loose, long coils

_____ 17. Pipe or tube to draw off or convey liquid

_____ 18. Pressing or urgent situations

_____ 19. Search made for useful military information in the field

_____ 20. Blocked with a defensive barrier

And Then There Were None Vocabulary Fill In The Blanks 1 Answer Key

VERISIMILITUDE	1. Appearance or semblance of truth; likelihood; probability
ABSTRACT	2. Theoretical; not applied or practical
FEASIBLE	3. Capable of being done, effected, or accomplished
PROVISIONED	4. Provided a stock of necessary supplies, especially food
CAIRNGORM	5. Smoky-yellow to dark brown or black variety of quartz, used as a gem stone
STILETTO	6. A small dagger with a slender, tapering blade
ADROITNESS	7. Expertise or nimbleness in the use of the hands or body
TENACIOUS	8. Holding fast; characterized by keeping a firm hold
DUBIOUSLY	9. In a doubtful manner
INEVITABILITY	10. Unable to be avoided, evaded, or escaped
LASSITUDE	11. Weariness of body or mind from strain; lack of energy
HITHERTO	12. Up to this time; until now
SAGACITY	13. Acuteness of mental discernment and soundness of judgment
ANGULARITIES	14. Sharp corners; angular outlines
LARDER	15. Room or place where food is stored; pantry
SKEINS	16. Lengths of thread or yarn wound in loose, long coils
SIPHON	17. Pipe or tube to draw off or convey liquid
EXIGENCIES	18. Pressing or urgent situations
RECONNAISSANCE	19. Search made for useful military information in the field
BARRICADED	20. Blocked with a defensive barrier

And Then There Were None Vocabulary Fill In The Blanks 2

_____ 1. Unable to be avoided, evaded, or escaped

_____ 2. Transmitting messages by reflecting sunlight

_____ 3. Theoretical; not applied or practical

_____ 4. In a calm, peaceful, or tranquil manner

_____ 5. Heavy, water-resistant fabric

_____ 6. Showing regard or respect

_____ 7. Gasoline

_____ 8. Thick and firm outer coat or covering

_____ 9. Disposition or bent, esp. of the mind or will; a liking or preference

_____ 10. False showing

_____ 11. Piece of dining room furniture having drawers and shelves for linens and tableware

_____ 12. Occurring or coming later or after

_____ 13. Lengths of thread or yarn wound in loose, long coils

_____ 14. Provided a stock of necessary supplies, especially food

_____ 15. Look or expression of the face

_____ 16. Undertaking involving uncertainty as to the outcome

_____ 17. Inflammation of the membrane surrounding the abdominal cavity

_____ 18. Having a slanting or sloping direction, course, or position

_____ 19. Sudden, short exclamations, especially brief pious utterances or prayers

_____ 20. Up to this time; until now

And Then There Were None Vocabulary Fill In The Blanks 2 Answer Key

INEVITABILITY	1. Unable to be avoided, evaded, or escaped
HELIOGRAPHING	2. Transmitting messages by reflecting sunlight
ABSTRACT	3. Theoretical; not applied or practical
SERENELY	4. In a calm, peaceful, or tranquil manner
OILSILK	5. Heavy, water-resistant fabric
DEFERENTIAL	6. Showing regard or respect
PETROL	7. Gasoline
RIND	8. Thick and firm outer coat or covering
INCLINATION	9. Disposition or bent, esp. of the mind or will; a liking or preference
PRETENCE	10. False showing
SIDEBOARD	11. Piece of dining room furniture having drawers and shelves for linens and tableware
SUBSEQUENT	12. Occurring or coming later or after
SKEINS	13. Lengths of thread or yarn wound in loose, long coils
PROVISIONED	14. Provided a stock of necessary supplies, especially food
COUNTENANCE	15. Look or expression of the face
VENTURE	16. Undertaking involving uncertainty as to the outcome
PERITONITIS	17. Inflammation of the membrane surrounding the abdominal cavity
OBLIQUELY	18. Having a slanting or sloping direction, course, or position
EJACULATIONS	19. Sudden, short exclamations, especially brief pious utterances or prayers
HITHERTO	20. Up to this time; until now

And Then There Were None Vocabulary Fill In The Blanks 3

_____ 1. Undertaking involving uncertainty as to the outcome

_____ 2. Theoretical; not applied or practical

_____ 3. Act of accusing in return

_____ 4. Thick and firm outer coat or covering

_____ 5. In a calm, peaceful, or tranquil manner

_____ 6. Gift of property or money through a will; a bequest

_____ 7. Disposition or bent, esp. of the mind or will; a liking or preference

_____ 8. Small tool for boring holes

_____ 9. In between period of time

_____ 10. Dose of liquid medicine

_____ 11. Disregarded; ignored

_____ 12. Physical or bodily structure; appearance

_____ 13. Sealed glass or plastic bulb containing solutions for hypodermic injection

_____ 14. Shrunk back, as in fear or repugnance

_____ 15. Blocked with a defensive barrier

_____ 16. State of being completely forgotten or unknown

_____ 17. Lacking in consistency or visible order; disconnected

_____ 18. A small dagger with a slender, tapering blade

_____ 19. Attitude expressing excessive attentiveness

_____ 20. Indefinitely long periods of time

And Then There Were None Vocabulary Fill In The Blanks 3 Answer Key

VENTURE	1.	Undertaking involving uncertainty as to the outcome
ABSTRACT	2.	Theoretical; not applied or practical
RECRIMINATION	3.	Act of accusing in return
RIND	4.	Thick and firm outer coat or covering
SERENELY	5.	In a calm, peaceful, or tranquil manner
LEGACY	6.	Gift of property or money through a will; a bequest
INCLINATION	7.	Disposition or bent, esp. of the mind or will; a liking or preference
GIMLET	8.	Small tool for boring holes
INTERVAL	9.	In between period of time
DRAUGHT	10.	Dose of liquid medicine
UNHEEDED	11.	Disregarded; ignored
PHYSIQUE	12.	Physical or bodily structure; appearance
AMPOULE	13.	Sealed glass or plastic bulb containing solutions for hypodermic injection
RECOILED	14.	Shrunk back, as in fear or repugnance
BARRICADED	15.	Blocked with a defensive barrier
OBLIVION	16.	State of being completely forgotten or unknown
DESULTORY	17.	Lacking in consistency or visible order; disconnected
STILETTO	18.	A small dagger with a slender, tapering blade
SOLICITUDE	19.	Attitude expressing excessive attentiveness
AEONS	20.	Indefinitely long periods of time

And Then There Were None Vocabulary Fill In The Blanks 4

1. Nurse in training who is undergoing a trial period
2. Mysterious in meaning; puzzling; ambiguous
3. Indefinitely long periods of time
4. Characterized by a hypocritical concern with virtue or religious devotion
5. Gift of property or money through a will; a bequest
6. In a friendly, cordial manner
7. Thick and firm outer coat or covering
8. Reflecting on over and over again; turning a matter over in the mind
9. Unoccupied; not leased to or occupied by a tenant
10. Harmless
11. Hard, non-resilient rubber formed by vulcanizing natural rubber
12. Was of the same opinion; agreed
13. Transmitting messages by reflecting sunlight
14. False showing
15. Crudely or irregularly fashioned verse, often of a humorous or burlesque nature
16. Heavy, water-resistant fabric
17. Look or expression of the face
18. Sharp corners; angular outlines
19. Of the highest kind, quality, or order; surpassing all else or others
20. Pressing or urgent situations

And Then There Were None Vocabulary Fill In The Blanks 4 Answer Key

PROBATIONER	1. Nurse in training who is undergoing a trial period
CRYPTIC	2. Mysterious in meaning; puzzling; ambiguous
AEONS	3. Indefinitely long periods of time
PIOUS	4. Characterized by a hypocritical concern with virtue or religious devotion
LEGACY	5. Gift of property or money through a will; a bequest
AFFABLY	6. In a friendly, cordial manner
RIND	7. Thick and firm outer coat or covering
RUMINATING	8. Reflecting on over and over again; turning a matter over in the mind
UNTENANTED	9. Unoccupied; not leased to or occupied by a tenant
INNOCUOUS	10. Harmless
EBONITE	11. Hard, non-resilient rubber formed by vulcanizing natural rubber
CONCURRED	12. Was of the same opinion; agreed
HELIOGRAPHING	13. Transmitting messages by reflecting sunlight
PRETENCE	14. False showing
DOGGEREL	15. Crudely or irregularly fashioned verse, often of a humorous or burlesque nature
OILSILK	16. Heavy, water-resistant fabric
COUNTENANCE	17. Look or expression of the face
ANGULARITIES	18. Sharp corners; angular outlines
SUPERLATIVELY	19. Of the highest kind, quality, or order; surpassing all else or others
EXIGENCIES	20. Pressing or urgent situations

And Then There Were None Vocabulary Matching 1

___ 1. SUFFUSED
___ 2. STILETTO
___ 3. DEPORTMENT
___ 4. CLAMBERED
___ 5. VERISIMILITUDE
___ 6. COUNTENANCE
___ 7. SUPERLATIVELY
___ 8. CRYPTIC
___ 9. ABSTRACT
___ 10. PROVISIONED
___ 11. OBLIVION
___ 12. HITHERTO
___ 13. SKEINS
___ 14. RECOILED
___ 15. REPROACH
___ 16. CONCURRED
___ 17. SAGACITY
___ 18. UNOBTRUSIVELY
___ 19. HELIOGRAPHING
___ 20. GIDDINESS
___ 21. INCLINATION
___ 22. PERITONITIS
___ 23. SIDEBOARD
___ 24. INNOCUOUS
___ 25. COVERTLY

A. State of being completely forgotten or unknown
B. Find fault with; blame; censure
C. Harmless
D. Mysterious in meaning; puzzling; ambiguous
E. Shrunk back, as in fear or repugnance
F. Appearance or semblance of truth; likelihood; probability
G. Was of the same opinion; agreed
H. Disposition or bent, esp. of the mind or will; a liking or preference
I. Acuteness of mental discernment and soundness of judgment
J. Theoretical; not applied or practical
K. Dizziness
L. Look or expression of the face
M. In a manner that is not undesirably noticeable or blatant
N. Secretly; in a concealed manner
O. Transmitting messages by reflecting sunlight
P. Inflammation of the membrane surrounding the abdominal cavity
Q. Provided a stock of necessary supplies, especially food
R. A small dagger with a slender, tapering blade
S. Piece of dining room furniture having drawers and shelves for linens and tableware
T. Up to this time; until now
U. Demeanor; conduct; behavior
V. Of the highest kind, quality, or order; surpassing all else or others
W. Climbed with difficulty, especially on all fours
X. Lengths of thread or yarn wound in loose, long coils
Y. Spread through or over, as with liquid, color, or light

And Then There Were None Vocabulary Matching 1 Answer Key

Y - 1. SUFFUSED
R - 2. STILETTO
U - 3. DEPORTMENT
W - 4. CLAMBERED
F - 5. VERISIMILITUDE
L - 6. COUNTENANCE
V - 7. SUPERLATIVELY
D - 8. CRYPTIC
J - 9. ABSTRACT
Q - 10. PROVISIONED
A - 11. OBLIVION
T - 12. HITHERTO
X - 13. SKEINS
E - 14. RECOILED
B - 15. REPROACH
G - 16. CONCURRED
I - 17. SAGACITY
M - 18. UNOBTRUSIVELY
O - 19. HELIOGRAPHING
K - 20. GIDDINESS
H - 21. INCLINATION
P - 22. PERITONITIS
S - 23. SIDEBOARD
C - 24. INNOCUOUS
N - 25. COVERTLY

A. State of being completely forgotten or unknown
B. Find fault with; blame; censure
C. Harmless
D. Mysterious in meaning; puzzling; ambiguous
E. Shrunk back, as in fear or repugnance
F. Appearance or semblance of truth; likelihood; probability
G. Was of the same opinion; agreed
H. Disposition or bent, esp. of the mind or will; a liking or preference
I. Acuteness of mental discernment and soundness of judgment
J. Theoretical; not applied or practical
K. Dizziness
L. Look or expression of the face
M. In a manner that is not undesirably noticeable or blatant
N. Secretly; in a concealed manner
O. Transmitting messages by reflecting sunlight
P. Inflammation of the membrane surrounding the abdominal cavity
Q. Provided a stock of necessary supplies, especially food
R. A small dagger with a slender, tapering blade
S. Piece of dining room furniture having drawers and shelves for linens and tableware
T. Up to this time; until now
U. Demeanor; conduct; behavior
V. Of the highest kind, quality, or order; surpassing all else or others
W. Climbed with difficulty, especially on all fours
X. Lengths of thread or yarn wound in loose, long coils
Y. Spread through or over, as with liquid, color, or light

Copyrighted

And Then There Were None Vocabulary Matching 2

___ 1. DESULTORY   A. Discharge or release from life
___ 2. VENTURE   B. Capable of being done, effected, or accomplished
___ 3. UNOBTRUSIVELY   C. In a manner that is not undesirably noticeable or blatant
___ 4. RUMINATING   D. In a friendly, cordial manner
___ 5. FEASIBLE   E. Harmless
___ 6. DOGGEREL   F. In an evil, harmful, or injurious manner
___ 7. INCLINATION   G. Reflecting on over and over again; turning a matter over in the mind
___ 8. OBLIVION   H. Raincoat
___ 9. AFFABLY   I. Lacking in consistency or visible order; disconnected
___10. MACKINTOSH   J. Weariness of body or mind from strain; lack of energy
___11. INNOCUOUS   K. Room or place where food is stored; pantry
___12. PETROL   L. Piece of dining room furniture having drawers and shelves for linens and tableware
___13. PACIFICALLY   M. Sudden, short exclamations, especially brief pious utterances or prayers
___14. LARDER   N. Having a slanting or sloping direction, course, or position
___15. ADROITNESS   O. Written statements charging a party with the commission of a crime
___16. MALEVOLENTLY   P. Expertise or nimbleness in the use of the hands or body
___17. OBLIQUELY   Q. In a calm, peaceful, or tranquil manner
___18. LASSITUDE   R. Gasoline
___19. INDICTMENTS   S. Inflammation of the membrane surrounding the abdominal cavity
___20. SERENELY   T. Death by choking, smothering, or suffocating
___21. PERITONITIS   U. Crudely or irregularly fashioned verse, often of a humorous or burlesque nature
___22. SIDEBOARD   V. State of being completely forgotten or unknown
___23. ASPHYXIATION   W. Peaceably, mildly, calmly, or quietly
___24. EJACULATIONS   X. Disposition or bent, esp. of the mind or will; a liking or preference
___25. QUIETUS   Y. Undertaking involving uncertainty as to the outcome

And Then There Were None Vocabulary Matching 2 Answer Key

I - 1. DESULTORY
Y - 2. VENTURE
C - 3. UNOBTRUSIVELY
G - 4. RUMINATING
B - 5. FEASIBLE
U - 6. DOGGEREL
X - 7. INCLINATION
V - 8. OBLIVION
D - 9. AFFABLY
H - 10. MACKINTOSH
E - 11. INNOCUOUS
R - 12. PETROL
W - 13. PACIFICALLY
K - 14. LARDER
P - 15. ADROITNESS
F - 16. MALEVOLENTLY
N - 17. OBLIQUELY
J - 18. LASSITUDE
O - 19. INDICTMENTS
Q - 20. SERENELY
S - 21. PERITONITIS
L - 22. SIDEBOARD
T - 23. ASPHYXIATION
M - 24. EJACULATIONS
A - 25. QUIETUS

A. Discharge or release from life
B. Capable of being done, effected, or accomplished
C. In a manner that is not undesirably noticeable or blatant
D. In a friendly, cordial manner
E. Harmless
F. In an evil, harmful, or injurious manner
G. Reflecting on over and over again; turning a matter over in the mind
H. Raincoat
I. Lacking in consistency or visible order; disconnected
J. Weariness of body or mind from strain; lack of energy
K. Room or place where food is stored; pantry
L. Piece of dining room furniture having drawers and shelves for linens and tableware
M. Sudden, short exclamations, especially brief pious utterances or prayers
N. Having a slanting or sloping direction, course, or position
O. Written statements charging a party with the commission of a crime
P. Expertise or nimbleness in the use of the hands or body
Q. In a calm, peaceful, or tranquil manner
R. Gasoline
S. Inflammation of the membrane surrounding the abdominal cavity
T. Death by choking, smothering, or suffocating
U. Crudely or irregularly fashioned verse, often of a humorous or burlesque nature
V. State of being completely forgotten or unknown
W. Peaceably, mildly, calmly, or quietly
X. Disposition or bent, esp. of the mind or will; a liking or preference
Y. Undertaking involving uncertainty as to the outcome

And Then There Were None Vocabulary Matching 3

___ 1. CONCURRED A. Wharf; landing pier
___ 2. MACKINTOSH B. In between period of time
___ 3. VERISIMILITUDE C. Appearance or semblance of truth; likelihood; probability
___ 4. COVERTLY D. Provided a stock of necessary supplies, especially food
___ 5. FEASIBLE E. In a manner that is not undesirably noticeable or blatant
___ 6. VENTURE F. Shrunk back, as in fear or repugnance
___ 7. IMPROMPTU G. Undertaking involving uncertainty as to the outcome
___ 8. SOLICITUDE H. Heavy, water-resistant fabric
___ 9. CONJURING I. False showing
___10. CAIRNGORM J. Attitude expressing excessive attentiveness
___11. DUBIOUSLY K. Investigation made by a coroner into the cause of a death
___12. PACIFICALLY L. Demeanor; conduct; behavior
___13. INTERVAL M. Capable of being done, effected, or accomplished
___14. UNOBTRUSIVELY N. Raincoat
___15. AMPOULE O. Pressing or urgent situations
___16. RECOILED P. In a doubtful manner
___17. INQUEST Q. Affecting or influencing as if by invocation or a magic spell
___18. UNTENANTED R. Made or done without previous preparation
___19. PRETENCE S. Mysterious in meaning; puzzling; ambiguous
___20. DEPORTMENT T. Unoccupied; not leased to or occupied by a tenant
___21. JETTY U. Sealed glass or plastic bulb containing solutions for hypodermic injection
___22. PROVISIONED V. Peaceably, mildly, calmly, or quietly
___23. EXIGENCIES W. Smoky-yellow to dark brown or black variety of quartz, used as a gem stone
___24. CRYPTIC X. Was of the same opinion; agreed
___25. OILSILK Y. Secretly; in a concealed manner

And Then There Were None Vocabulary Matching 3 Answer Key

X - 1. CONCURRED
N - 2. MACKINTOSH
C - 3. VERISIMILITUDE
Y - 4. COVERTLY
M - 5. FEASIBLE
G - 6. VENTURE
R - 7. IMPROMPTU
J - 8. SOLICITUDE
Q - 9. CONJURING
W - 10. CAIRNGORM
P - 11. DUBIOUSLY
V - 12. PACIFICALLY
B - 13. INTERVAL
E - 14. UNOBTRUSIVELY
U - 15. AMPOULE
F - 16. RECOILED
K - 17. INQUEST
T - 18. UNTENANTED
I - 19. PRETENCE
L - 20. DEPORTMENT
A - 21. JETTY
D - 22. PROVISIONED
O - 23. EXIGENCIES
S - 24. CRYPTIC
H - 25. OILSILK

A. Wharf; landing pier
B. In between period of time
C. Appearance or semblance of truth; likelihood; probability
D. Provided a stock of necessary supplies, especially food
E. In a manner that is not undesirably noticeable or blatant
F. Shrunk back, as in fear or repugnance
G. Undertaking involving uncertainty as to the outcome
H. Heavy, water-resistant fabric
I. False showing
J. Attitude expressing excessive attentiveness
K. Investigation made by a coroner into the cause of a death
L. Demeanor; conduct; behavior
M. Capable of being done, effected, or accomplished
N. Raincoat
O. Pressing or urgent situations
P. In a doubtful manner
Q. Affecting or influencing as if by invocation or a magic spell
R. Made or done without previous preparation
S. Mysterious in meaning; puzzling; ambiguous
T. Unoccupied; not leased to or occupied by a tenant
U. Sealed glass or plastic bulb containing solutions for hypodermic injection
V. Peaceably, mildly, calmly, or quietly
W. Smoky-yellow to dark brown or black variety of quartz, used as a gem stone
X. Was of the same opinion; agreed
Y. Secretly; in a concealed manner

And Then There Were None Vocabulary Matching 4

___ 1. PRETENCE
___ 2. RECRIMINATION
___ 3. PETROL
___ 4. SKEINS
___ 5. UNTENANTED
___ 6. PALPABLY
___ 7. PIOUS
___ 8. EBONITE
___ 9. CONCLAVE
___ 10. GIDDINESS
___ 11. INQUEST
___ 12. MALEVOLENTLY
___ 13. IMPROMPTU
___ 14. REPROACH
___ 15. HELIOGRAPHING
___ 16. PACIFICALLY
___ 17. PERITONITIS
___ 18. CONCURRED
___ 19. CRYPTIC
___ 20. SIPHON
___ 21. MACKINTOSH
___ 22. INTERVAL
___ 23. INDICTMENTS
___ 24. CHANCERY
___ 25. ABSTRACT

A. Private or secret meeting
B. Transmitting messages by reflecting sunlight
C. Division of the High Court of Justice of Great Britain
D. Written statements charging a party with the commission of a crime
E. False showing
F. Investigation made by a coroner into the cause of a death
G. Was of the same opinion; agreed
H. Dizziness
I. In an evil, harmful, or injurious manner
J. Inflammation of the membrane surrounding the abdominal cavity
K. Unoccupied; not leased to or occupied by a tenant
L. Peaceably, mildly, calmly, or quietly
M. Lengths of thread or yarn wound in loose, long coils
N. Hard, non-resilient rubber formed by vulcanizing natural rubber
O. Act of accusing in return
P. Pipe or tube to draw off or convey liquid
Q. Theoretical; not applied or practical
R. In between period of time
S. Raincoat
T. Gasoline
U. Made or done without previous preparation
V. Find fault with; blame; censure
W. Plainly seen, heard, or perceived; obviously
X. Mysterious in meaning; puzzling; ambiguous
Y. Characterized by a hypocritical concern with virtue or religious devotion

And Then There Were None Vocabulary Matching 4 Answer Key

E - 1. PRETENCE	A. Private or secret meeting
O - 2. RECRIMINATION	B. Transmitting messages by reflecting sunlight
T - 3. PETROL	C. Division of the High Court of Justice of Great Britain
M - 4. SKEINS	D. Written statements charging a party with the commission of a crime
K - 5. UNTENANTED	E. False showing
W - 6. PALPABLY	F. Investigation made by a coroner into the cause of a death
Y - 7. PIOUS	G. Was of the same opinion; agreed
N - 8. EBONITE	H. Dizziness
A - 9. CONCLAVE	I. In an evil, harmful, or injurious manner
H - 10. GIDDINESS	J. Inflammation of the membrane surrounding the abdominal cavity
F - 11. INQUEST	K. Unoccupied; not leased to or occupied by a tenant
I - 12. MALEVOLENTLY	L. Peaceably, mildly, calmly, or quietly
U - 13. IMPROMPTU	M. Lengths of thread or yarn wound in loose, long coils
V - 14. REPROACH	N. Hard, non-resilient rubber formed by vulcanizing natural rubber
B - 15. HELIOGRAPHING	O. Act of accusing in return
L - 16. PACIFICALLY	P. Pipe or tube to draw off or convey liquid
J - 17. PERITONITIS	Q. Theoretical; not applied or practical
G - 18. CONCURRED	R. In between period of time
X - 19. CRYPTIC	S. Raincoat
P - 20. SIPHON	T. Gasoline
S - 21. MACKINTOSH	U. Made or done without previous preparation
R - 22. INTERVAL	V. Find fault with; blame; censure
D - 23. INDICTMENTS	W. Plainly seen, heard, or perceived; obviously
C - 24. CHANCERY	X. Mysterious in meaning; puzzling; ambiguous
Q - 25. ABSTRACT	Y. Characterized by a hypocritical concern with virtue or religious devotion

And Then There Were None Vocabulary Magic Squares 1

Match the definition with the vocabulary word. Put your answers in the magic squares below. When your answers are correct, all columns and rows will add to the same number.

A. ASPHYXIATION
B. COVERTLY
C. DEFERENTIAL
D. ADROITNESS
E. ABSTRACT
F. UNTENANTED
G. LASSITUDE
H. HITHERTO
I. EJACULATIONS
J. COUNTENANCE
K. ANGULARITIES
L. INTERVAL
M. AMPOULE
N. GIDDINESS
O. MALICIOUS
P. AUTOMATON

1. Sealed glass or plastic bulb containing solutions for hypodermic injection
2. Unoccupied; not leased to or occupied by a tenant
3. Up to this time; until now
4. Deliberately harmful or spiteful
5. In between period of time
6. Showing regard or respect
7. Death by choking, smothering, or suffocating
8. Look or expression of the face
9. Sharp corners; angular outlines
10. Expertise or nimbleness in the use of the hands or body
11. Secretly; in a concealed manner
12. Sudden, short exclamations, especially brief pious utterances or prayers
13. Dizziness
14. Theoretical; not applied or practical
15. Weariness of body or mind from strain; lack of energy
16. Mechanical figure; robot

A=	B=	C=	D=
E=	F=	G=	H=
I=	J=	K=	L=
M=	N=	O=	P=

And Then There Were None Vocabulary Magic Squares 1 Answer Key

Match the definition with the vocabulary word. Put your answers in the magic squares below. When your answers are correct, all columns and rows will add to the same number.

A. ASPHYXIATION
B. COVERTLY
C. DEFERENTIAL
D. ADROITNESS
E. ABSTRACT
F. UNTENANTED
G. LASSITUDE
H. HITHERTO
I. EJACULATIONS
J. COUNTENANCE
K. ANGULARITIES
L. INTERVAL
M. AMPOULE
N. GIDDINESS
O. MALICIOUS
P. AUTOMATON

1. Sealed glass or plastic bulb containing solutions for hypodermic injection
2. Unoccupied; not leased to or occupied by a tenant
3. Up to this time; until now
4. Deliberately harmful or spiteful
5. In between period of time
6. Showing regard or respect
7. Death by choking, smothering, or suffocating
8. Look or expression of the face
9. Sharp corners; angular outlines
10. Expertise or nimbleness in the use of the hands or body
11. Secretly; in a concealed manner
12. Sudden, short exclamations, especially brief pious utterances or prayers
13. Dizziness
14. Theoretical; not applied or practical
15. Weariness of body or mind from strain; lack of energy
16. Mechanical figure; robot

A=7	B=11	C=6	D=10
E=14	F=2	G=15	H=3
I=12	J=8	K=9	L=5
M=1	N=13	O=4	P=16

And Then There Were None Vocabulary Magic Squares 2

Match the definition with the vocabulary word. Put your answers in the magic squares below. When your answers are correct, all columns and rows will add to the same number.

A. ANGULARITIES
B. CAIRNGORM
C. VENTURE
D. CRYPTIC
E. INTERVAL
F. MALICIOUS
G. SKEINS
H. SERENELY
I. VERISIMILITUDE
J. DESULTORY
K. STILETTO
L. OBLIVION
M. JETTY
N. INEVITABILITY
O. HELIOGRAPHING
P. SUBSEQUENT

1. Unable to be avoided, evaded, or escaped
2. Lengths of thread or yarn wound in loose, long coils
3. State of being completely forgotten or unknown
4. Sharp corners; angular outlines
5. A small dagger with a slender, tapering blade
6. Smoky-yellow to dark brown or black variety of quartz, used as a gem stone
7. Wharf; landing pier
8. In a calm, peaceful, or tranquil manner
9. In between period of time
10. Occurring or coming later or after
11. Undertaking involving uncertainty as to the outcome
12. Lacking in consistency or visible order; disconnected
13. Mysterious in meaning; puzzling; ambiguous
14. Appearance or semblance of truth; likelihood; probability
15. Deliberately harmful or spiteful
16. Transmitting messages by reflecting sunlight

A=	B=	C=	D=
E=	F=	G=	H=
I=	J=	K=	L=
M=	N=	O=	P=

And Then There Were None Vocabulary Magic Squares 2 Answer Key

Match the definition with the vocabulary word. Put your answers in the magic squares below. When your answers are correct, all columns and rows will add to the same number.

A. ANGULARITIES
B. CAIRNGORM
C. VENTURE
D. CRYPTIC
E. INTERVAL
F. MALICIOUS
G. SKEINS
H. SERENELY
I. VERISIMILITUDE
J. DESULTORY
K. STILETTO
L. OBLIVION
M. JETTY
N. INEVITABILITY
O. HELIOGRAPHING
P. SUBSEQUENT

1. Unable to be avoided, evaded, or escaped
2. Lengths of thread or yarn wound in loose, long coils
3. State of being completely forgotten or unknown
4. Sharp corners; angular outlines
5. A small dagger with a slender, tapering blade
6. Smoky-yellow to dark brown or black variety of quartz, used as a gem stone
7. Wharf; landing pier
8. In a calm, peaceful, or tranquil manner
9. In between period of time
10. Occurring or coming later or after
11. Undertaking involving uncertainty as to the outcome
12. Lacking in consistency or visible order; disconnected
13. Mysterious in meaning; puzzling; ambiguous
14. Appearance or semblance of truth; likelihood; probability
15. Deliberately harmful or spiteful
16. Transmitting messages by reflecting sunlight

A=4	B=6	C=11	D=13
E=9	F=15	G=2	H=8
I=14	J=12	K=5	L=3
M=7	N=1	O=16	P=10

And Then There Were None Vocabulary Magic Squares 3

Match the definition with the vocabulary word. Put your answers in the magic squares below. When your answers are correct, all columns and rows will add to the same number.

A. PRETENCE
B. UNOBTRUSIVELY
C. RUMINATING
D. VENTURE
E. EXIGENCIES
F. PROVISIONED
G. MALICIOUS
H. DEPORTMENT
I. QUIETUS
J. ABSTRACT
K. INDICTMENTS
L. EBONITE
M. SUFFUSED
N. SIPHON
O. UNHEEDED
P. ABHORRENT

1. False showing
2. Pipe or tube to draw off or convey liquid
3. Theoretical; not applied or practical
4. Pressing or urgent situations
5. Deliberately harmful or spiteful
6. Hard, non-resilient rubber formed by vulcanizing natural rubber
7. Detestable; loathsome; hateful
8. Reflecting on over and over again; turning a matter over in the mind
9. Disregarded; ignored
10. Undertaking involving uncertainty as to the outcome
11. Demeanor; conduct; behavior
12. Written statements charging a party with the commission of a crime
13. Discharge or release from life
14. Provided a stock of necessary supplies, especially food
15. In a manner that is not undesirably noticeable or blatant
16. Spread through or over, as with liquid, color, or light

A=	B=	C=	D=
E=	F=	G=	H=
I=	J=	K=	L=
M=	N=	O=	P=

And Then There Were None Vocabulary Magic Squares 3 Answer Key

Match the definition with the vocabulary word. Put your answers in the magic squares below. When your answers are correct, all columns and rows will add to the same number.

A. PRETENCE
B. UNOBTRUSIVELY
C. RUMINATING
D. VENTURE
E. EXIGENCIES
F. PROVISIONED

G. MALICIOUS
H. DEPORTMENT
I. QUIETUS
J. ABSTRACT
K. INDICTMENTS
L. EBONITE

M. SUFFUSED
N. SIPHON
O. UNHEEDED
P. ABHORRENT

1. False showing
2. Pipe or tube to draw off or convey liquid
3. Theoretical; not applied or practical
4. Pressing or urgent situations
5. Deliberately harmful or spiteful
6. Hard, non-resilient rubber formed by vulcanizing natural rubber
7. Detestable; loathsome; hateful
8. Reflecting on over and over again; turning a matter over in the mind
9. Disregarded; ignored
10. Undertaking involving uncertainty as to the outcome
11. Demeanor; conduct; behavior
12. Written statements charging a party with the commission of a crime
13. Discharge or release from life
14. Provided a stock of necessary supplies, especially food
15. In a manner that is not undesirably noticeable or blatant
16. Spread through or over, as with liquid, color, or light

A=1	B=15	C=8	D=10
E=4	F=14	G=5	H=11
I=13	J=3	K=12	L=6
M=16	N=2	O=9	P=7

And Then There Were None Vocabulary Magic Squares 4

Match the definition with the vocabulary word. Put your answers in the magic squares below. When your answers are correct, all columns and rows will add to the same number.

A. CHANCERY
B. RUMINATING
C. MACKINTOSH
D. DUBIOUSLY
E. INNOCUOUS
F. SUPERLATIVELY
G. ADMONITORY
H. CRYPTIC
I. PHYSIQUE
J. RIND
K. PALPABLY
L. DEPORTMENT
M. COUNTENANCE
N. LASSITUDE
O. INCLINATION
P. CONCLAVE

1. Mysterious in meaning; puzzling; ambiguous
2. Division of the High Court of Justice of Great Britain
3. Reflecting on over and over again; turning a matter over in the mind
4. Serving to warn, especially to correct
5. Thick and firm outer coat or covering
6. Disposition or bent, esp. of the mind or will; a liking or preference
7. Private or secret meeting
8. Physical or bodily structure; appearance
9. Plainly seen, heard, or perceived; obviously
10. Weariness of body or mind from strain; lack of energy
11. Look or expression of the face
12. Demeanor; conduct; behavior
13. Harmless
14. In a doubtful manner
15. Raincoat
16. Of the highest kind, quality, or order; surpassing all else or others

A=	B=	C=	D=
E=	F=	G=	H=
I=	J=	K=	L=
M=	N=	O=	P=

And Then There Were None Vocabulary Magic Squares 4 Answer Key

Match the definition with the vocabulary word. Put your answers in the magic squares below. When your answers are correct, all columns and rows will add to the same number.

A. CHANCERY
B. RUMINATING
C. MACKINTOSH
D. DUBIOUSLY
E. INNOCUOUS
F. SUPERLATIVELY
G. ADMONITORY
H. CRYPTIC
I. PHYSIQUE
J. RIND
K. PALPABLY
L. DEPORTMENT
M. COUNTENANCE
N. LASSITUDE
O. INCLINATION
P. CONCLAVE

1. Mysterious in meaning; puzzling; ambiguous
2. Division of the High Court of Justice of Great Britain
3. Reflecting on over and over again; turning a matter over in the mind
4. Serving to warn, especially to correct
5. Thick and firm outer coat or covering
6. Disposition or bent, esp. of the mind or will; a liking or preference
7. Private or secret meeting
8. Physical or bodily structure; appearance
9. Plainly seen, heard, or perceived; obviously
10. Weariness of body or mind from strain; lack of energy
11. Look or expression of the face
12. Demeanor; conduct; behavior
13. Harmless
14. In a doubtful manner
15. Raincoat
16. Of the highest kind, quality, or order; surpassing all else or others

A=2	B=3	C=15	D=14
E=13	F=16	G=4	H=1
I=8	J=5	K=9	L=12
M=11	N=10	O=6	P=7

And Then There Were None Vocabulary Word Search 1

```
D T Y M A M P O U L E S N E K P R S Y V
C U L C O V E R T L Y I U S B R U H L W
H V B Y R O T L U S E D N I R O I E E S
A E A I L A R D E R E E O M I B N L V X
N R F T O P O N J R D B B P E A T I I Z
C I F M K U L C E S U O T R X T E O T K
E S A R L D S B T K T A R O I I R G A E
R I B B I R M L T E I R U M G O V R L W
Y M H N S A E N Y I S D S P E N A A R D
R I O G L T V P S N S T I T N E L P E S
E L R C I Q R U R S A E V U C R P H P T
C I R K O G T A J O L N E I I S A I U Q
O T E J L E G A C Y A A L N E I L N S F
I U N H I N E R T T R C Y Q S P P G G V
L D T U F O T R E H T I H U K H A W R R
E E Q A E O N S J K D O L E W O B Y J K
D S O L I C I T U D E U L S S N L L A P
R U M I N A T I N G J S M T V Y Y M D H
```

Anything that covers, shrouds, or overspreads, esp. with darkness or gloom (4)
Appearance or semblance of truth; likelihood; probability (14)
Attitude expressing excessive attentiveness (10)
Characterized by a hypocritical concern with virtue or religious devotion (5)
Climbed with difficulty, especially on all fours (9)
Detestable; loathsome; hateful (9)
Discharge or release from life (7)
Division of the High Court of Justice of Great Britain (8)
Find fault with; blame; censure (8)
Gasoline (6)
Gift of property or money through a will; a bequest (6)
Hard, non-resilient rubber formed by vulcanizing natural rubber (7)
Heavy, water-resistant fabric (7)
Holding fast; characterized by keeping a firm hold (9)
In a doubtful manner (9)
In a friendly, cordial manner (7)
In a manner that is not undesirably noticeable or blatant (13)
In between period of time (8)
Indefinitely long periods of time (5)
Investigation made by a coroner into the cause of a death (7)

Lacking in consistency or visible order; disconnected (9)
Lengths of thread or yarn wound in loose, long coils (6)
Made or done without previous preparation (9)
Nurse in training who is undergoing a trial period (11)
Of the highest kind, quality, or order; surpassing all else or others (13)
Piece of dining room furniture having drawers and shelves for linens and tableware (9)
Pipe or tube to draw off or convey liquid (6)
Plainly seen, heard, or perceived; obviously (8)
Pressing or urgent situations (10)
Reflecting on over and over again; turning a matter over in the mind (10)
Room or place where food is stored; pantry (6)
Sealed glass or plastic bulb containing solutions for hypodermic injection (7)
Secretly; in a concealed manner (8)
Shrunk back, as in fear or repugnance (8)
Theoretical; not applied or practical (8)
Thick and firm outer coat or covering (4)
Transmitting messages by reflecting sunlight (13)
Unable to move or act (5)
Up to this time; until now (8)
Weariness of body or mind from strain; lack of energy (9)
Wharf; landing pier (5)

And Then There Were None Vocabulary Word Search 1 Answer Key

```
D       Y       A  M  P  O  U  L  E  S     E     P     S  Y
C  U  L  C  O  V  E  R  T  L  Y  I     U     B  R  U  H  L
H  V  B  Y  R  O  T  L  U  S  E  D  N  I  R  O  I  E  E
A  E  A  I  L  A  R  D  E  R  E  E  O  M  I  B  N  L  V
N  R  F     O     O     J  R  D  B  P  E  A  T  I  I
C  I  F     K  U  L     E  S  U  O  T  R  X  T  E  O  T
E  S  A     L     S  B  T  K  T  A  R  O  I  I  R  G  A   E
R  I  B  B  I  R  M  L  T  E  I  R  U  M  G  O  V  R  L
Y  M  H     S  A  E     Y  I  S  D  S  P  E  N  A  A  R
R  I  O     L  T     P  S  N  S  T  I  T  N  E  L  P  E
E  L  R  C  I     R  U  R  S  A  O  L  N  C  R  P  H  P
C  R  R     O     T  A     O  L  N  E  I  I  S  A  I  U
O  T  E     L  E  G  A  C  Y  A  A     E  I  L  L  N  S
I  U  N     N  E  R  T  T     C  Y  Q  S  P  P  G
L  D  T  U     O  T  R  E  H  T  I  H  U  H  A
E  E  Q  A  E  O  N  S        O     E  O  B
D  S  O  L  I  C  I  T  U  D  E  U     S  N  L  A  P
R  U  M  I  N  A  T  I  N  G     S     T     Y
```

Anything that covers, shrouds, or overspreads, esp. with darkness or gloom (4)
Appearance or semblance of truth; likelihood; probability (14)
Attitude expressing excessive attentiveness (10)
Characterized by a hypocritical concern with virtue or religious devotion (5)
Climbed with difficulty, especially on all fours (9)
Detestable; loathsome; hateful (9)
Discharge or release from life (7)
Division of the High Court of Justice of Great Britain (8)
Find fault with; blame; censure (8)
Gasoline (6)
Gift of property or money through a will; a bequest (6)
Hard, non-resilient rubber formed by vulcanizing natural rubber (7)
Heavy, water-resistant fabric (7)
Holding fast; characterized by keeping a firm hold (9)
In a doubtful manner (9)
In a friendly, cordial manner (7)
In a manner that is not undesirably noticeable or blatant (13)
In between period of time (8)
Indefinitely long periods of time (5)
Investigation made by a coroner into the cause of a death (7)
Lacking in consistency or visible order; disconnected (9)
Lengths of thread or yarn wound in loose, long coils (6)
Made or done without previous preparation (9)
Nurse in training who is undergoing a trial period (11)
Of the highest kind, quality, or order; surpassing all else or others (13)
Piece of dining room furniture having drawers and shelves for linens and tableware (9)
Pipe or tube to draw off or convey liquid (6)
Plainly seen, heard, or perceived; obviously (8)
Pressing or urgent situations (10)
Reflecting on over and over again; turning a matter over in the mind (10)
Room or place where food is stored; pantry (6)
Sealed glass or plastic bulb containing solutions for hypodermic injection (7)
Secretly; in a concealed manner (8)
Shrunk back, as in fear or repugnance (8)
Theoretical; not applied or practical (8)
Thick and firm outer coat or covering (4)
Transmitting messages by reflecting sunlight (13)
Unable to move or act (5)
Up to this time; until now (8)
Weariness of body or mind from strain; lack of energy (9)
Wharf; landing pier (5)

And Then There Were None Vocabulary Word Search 2

```
A S I P H O N S T I L E T T O N S M Y I
F S N A I Y H P T K P H E T O R A C N B
F U Q L L O C P S A G L T I G C A T T S
A O U L A C U Q K U M S V X K G E N A C
B I E S S H G S A I W I R I E R E C N N
L C S I S A I R G A L E N L V M G D G N
Y I T D I N D G N B D T N A T D E L U Y
S L B E T C D P O R O R L R U N Y Y L K
E A K B U E I A A S Z H O B O Q R Y A P
R M G O D R N L H X T P I I D O R J R B
E J S A E Y E P M B E O S E T O J G I X
N P K R C R S A T D U I R I T N J S T M
E G E D U I S B R S V R N L S K E T I F
L I I T R B T L L O U O R K V T S E D
Y P N C I T P Y R C M S Q U I E T U S G
W E S E K L X P N D E E Q I S Y H P J
V P E T R O L O A D E D E E H N U K K G
A E O N S T C L A M B E R E D R I N D N
```

Acuteness of mental discernment and soundness of judgment (8)
Anything that covers, shrouds, or overspreads, esp. with darkness or gloom (4)
Characterized by a hypocritical concern with virtue or religious devotion (5)
Climbed with difficulty, especially on all fours (9)
Deliberately harmful or spiteful (9)
Demeanor; conduct; behavior (10)
Discharge or release from life (7)
Disregarded; ignored (8)
Division of the High Court of Justice of Great Britain (8)
Dizziness (9)
Dose of liquid medicine (7)
Expertise or nimbleness in the use of the hands or body (10)
Gasoline (6)
Gift of property or money through a will; a bequest (6)
In a calm, peaceful, or tranquil manner (8)
In a doubtful manner (9)
In a friendly, cordial manner (7)
In between period of time (8)
Indefinitely long periods of time (5)
Investigation made by a coroner into the cause of a death (7)
Lacking in consistency or visible order; disconnected (9)

Lengths of thread or yarn wound in loose, long coils (6)
Mysterious in meaning; puzzling; ambiguous (7)
Physical or bodily structure; appearance (8)
Physical or moral strength to resist or withstand illness, fatigue, or hardship; endurance (7)
Piece of dining room furniture having drawers and shelves for linens and tableware (9)
Pipe or tube to draw off or convey liquid (6)
Plainly seen, heard, or perceived; obviously (8)
Provided a stock of necessary supplies, especially food (11)
Raincoat (10)
Room or place where food is stored; pantry (6)
Serving to warn, especially to correct (10)
Sharp corners; angular outlines (12)
A small dagger with a slender, tapering blade (8)
Small tool for boring holes (6)
State of being completely forgotten or unknown (8)
Thick and firm outer coat or covering (4)
Unable to move or act (5)
Undertaking involving uncertainty as to the outcome (7)
Was of the same opinion; agreed (9)
Weariness of body or mind from strain; lack of energy (9)
Wharf; landing pier (5)

And Then There Were None Vocabulary Word Search 2 Answer Key

[word search grid]

- Acuteness of mental discernment and soundness of judgment (8)
- Anything that covers, shrouds, or overspreads, esp. with darkness or gloom (4)
- Characterized by a hypocritical concern with virtue or religious devotion (5)
- Climbed with difficulty, especially on all fours (9)
- Deliberately harmful or spiteful (9)
- Demeanor; conduct; behavior (10)
- Discharge or release from life (7)
- Disregarded; ignored (8)
- Division of the High Court of Justice of Great Britain (8)
- Dizziness (9)
- Dose of liquid medicine (7)
- Expertise or nimbleness in the use of the hands or body (10)
- Gasoline (6)
- Gift of property or money through a will; a bequest (6)
- In a calm, peaceful, or tranquil manner (8)
- In a doubtful manner (9)
- In a friendly, cordial manner (7)
- In between period of time (8)
- Indefinitely long periods of time (5)
- Investigation made by a coroner into the cause of a death (7)
- Lacking in consistency or visible order; disconnected (9)
- Lengths of thread or yarn wound in loose, long coils (6)
- Mysterious in meaning; puzzling; ambiguous (7)
- Physical or bodily structure; appearance (8)
- Physical or moral strength to resist or withstand illness, fatigue, or hardship; endurance (7)
- Piece of dining room furniture having drawers and shelves for linens and tableware (9)
- Pipe or tube to draw off or convey liquid (6)
- Plainly seen, heard, or perceived; obviously (8)
- Provided a stock of necessary supplies, especially food (11)
- Raincoat (10)
- Room or place where food is stored; pantry (6)
- Serving to warn, especially to correct (10)
- Sharp corners; angular outlines (12)
- A small dagger with a slender, tapering blade (8)
- Small tool for boring holes (6)
- State of being completely forgotten or unknown (8)
- Thick and firm outer coat or covering (4)
- Unable to move or act (5)
- Undertaking involving uncertainty as to the outcome (7)
- Was of the same opinion; agreed (9)
- Weariness of body or mind from strain; lack of energy (9)
- Wharf; landing pier (5)

And Then There Were None Vocabulary Word Search 3

```
C D U B I O U S L Y O B L I V I O N R M
O Y X D N X E U C E C N A N E T N U O C
V L X V R R T L S U O I N C A N U G W
E T V M E U E A V O S N D R N E T H
R N S N D G T I M Q N L E C N E R P
T E E F R D N U B I R M I X L B U K Y
L L D E A E E Q E K R C F C Z A M X S B
Y O E A L D V K S T R Q P I V H U C
T V F S B E S T E L J Y M L N T R E O Q
T E E I R E O I D L Y P H A Y B U T D S
E L R B N H C I B L P T T F R S Y D N F
J A E L A N G U L A R I T I E S N O E A
J M N E E U O A Y S N C O L K U R G P Z
R K T G D Y C C C G I M Y U V O E G U N
Q W I V P I E Y U N R L G W S I C E T M
V X A L F L T V T O K I K I T C O R S V
E S L I U I Y R G H U N N S M I I E M V
Q G C O C C E N V P V S E D M L L L C D
Q A P A A N R R T I H U V P P A E V B V
P M G G I I D G K S Q Q P A N M D T W Z
A A E L A V R E T N I O B L I Q U E L Y
S L D C G I D D I N E S S L O R T E P W
```

AEONS	DUBIOUSLY	MALEVOLENTLY	RIND
AMPOULE	EXIGENCIES	MALICIOUS	RUMINATING
ANGULARITIES	FEASIBLE	OBLIQUELY	SAGACITY
CAIRNGORM	GIDDINESS	OBLIVION	SERENELY
CLAMBERED	GIMLET	OILSILK	SIPHON
CONCLAVE	INERT	PACIFICALLY	SKEINS
COUNTENANCE	INNOCUOUS	PALL	SOLICITUDE
COVERTLY	INQUEST	PETROL	STUPENDOUS
CRYPTIC	INTERVAL	PIOUS	TENACIOUS
DEFERENTIAL	JETTY	PRETENCE	UNHEEDED
DOGGEREL	LARDER	QUIETUS	VENTURE
DRAUGHT	LEGACY	RECOILED	

And Then There Were None Vocabulary Word Search 3 Answer Key

AEONS	DUBIOUSLY	MALEVOLENTLY	RIND
AMPOULE	EXIGENCIES	MALICIOUS	RUMINATING
ANGULARITIES	FEASIBLE	OBLIQUELY	SAGACITY
CAIRNGORM	GIDDINESS	OBLIVION	SERENELY
CLAMBERED	GIMLET	OILSILK	SIPHON
CONCLAVE	INERT	PACIFICALLY	SKEINS
COUNTENANCE	INNOCUOUS	PALL	SOLICITUDE
COVERTLY	INQUEST	PETROL	STUPENDOUS
CRYPTIC	INTERVAL	PIOUS	TENACIOUS
DEFERENTIAL	JETTY	PRETENCE	UNHEEDED
DOGGEREL	LARDER	QUIETUS	VENTURE
DRAUGHT	LEGACY	RECOILED	

And Then There Were None Vocabulary Word Search 4

```
A U T O M A T O N E L E R E G G O D R Y
R N C Y M Y H M R C C D P L N Q P E U P
Y L R T H L I U M N S U H J I S D N T
R A Y P S E T S E A I T Y O T R E E R
E V P R S N H T B N P I S B A I S H N J
C R T E E E E U O E H S I L N M U N C
N E I V M R P N T O S Q I I P F A P
A T C O P E T E I N N A U V M R U T J
H N D C C S T O D T U Q L E I U O D T F
C I G E W L F D E O R S J O R M S W E N
T J K U S F S O R C N W J N R P X K D M
G E Z P L U W U R O T T E L I T S R R Z
K T S E B A L S I G I M L E T U A D E B
C T T T Q R T S E U Q N I K O U R C F
L Y A R H H A I O V T E R B B P E O S
A R M O G L S P T R L L Q E I L A P I M
M I I L U P K Z E I Y B D O S E L R L C
B N N C A I E N Y M E I U P Q G P O E V
E D A D R O I T N E S S N O E A A A D H
R J H F D U N T Q T L A S Y L C B C C M
E X Y H V S S R S Y C E M L G Y L H K X
D E P O R T M E N T A F F A B L Y Q S N
```

ADROITNESS	DEPORTMENT	IMPROMPTU	PALPABLY	SIDEBOARD
AEONS	DESULTORY	INERT	PETROL	SIPHON
AFFABLY	DOGGEREL	INQUEST	PHYSIQUE	SKEINS
ANGULARITIES	DRAUGHT	INTERVAL	PIOUS	STAMINA
AUTOMATON	DUBIOUSLY	JETTY	PRETENCE	STILETTO
CHANCERY	EBONITE	LARDER	RECOILED	STUPENDOUS
CLAMBERED	EJACULATIONS	LASSITUDE	REPROACH	SUFFUSED
COUNTENANCE	FEASIBLE	LEGACY	RIND	UNHEEDED
COVERTLY	GIMLET	OBLIVION	RUMINATING	UNTENANTED
CRYPTIC	HITHERTO	PALL	SERENELY	VENTURE

And Then There Were None Vocabulary Word Search 4 Answer Key

ADROITNESS	DEPORTMENT	IMPROMPTU	PALPABLY	SIDEBOARD
AEONS	DESULTORY	INERT	PETROL	SIPHON
AFFABLY	DOGGEREL	INQUEST	PHYSIQUE	SKEINS
ANGULARITIES	DRAUGHT	INTERVAL	PIOUS	STAMINA
AUTOMATON	DUBIOUSLY	JETTY	PRETENCE	STILETTO
CHANCERY	EBONITE	LARDER	RECOILED	STUPENDOUS
CLAMBERED	EJACULATIONS	LASSITUDE	REPROACH	SUFFUSED
COUNTENANCE	FEASIBLE	LEGACY	RIND	UNHEEDED
COVERTLY	GIMLET	OBLIVION	RUMINATING	UNTENANTED
CRYPTIC	HITHERTO	PALL	SERENELY	VENTURE

And Then There Were None Vocabulary Crossword 1

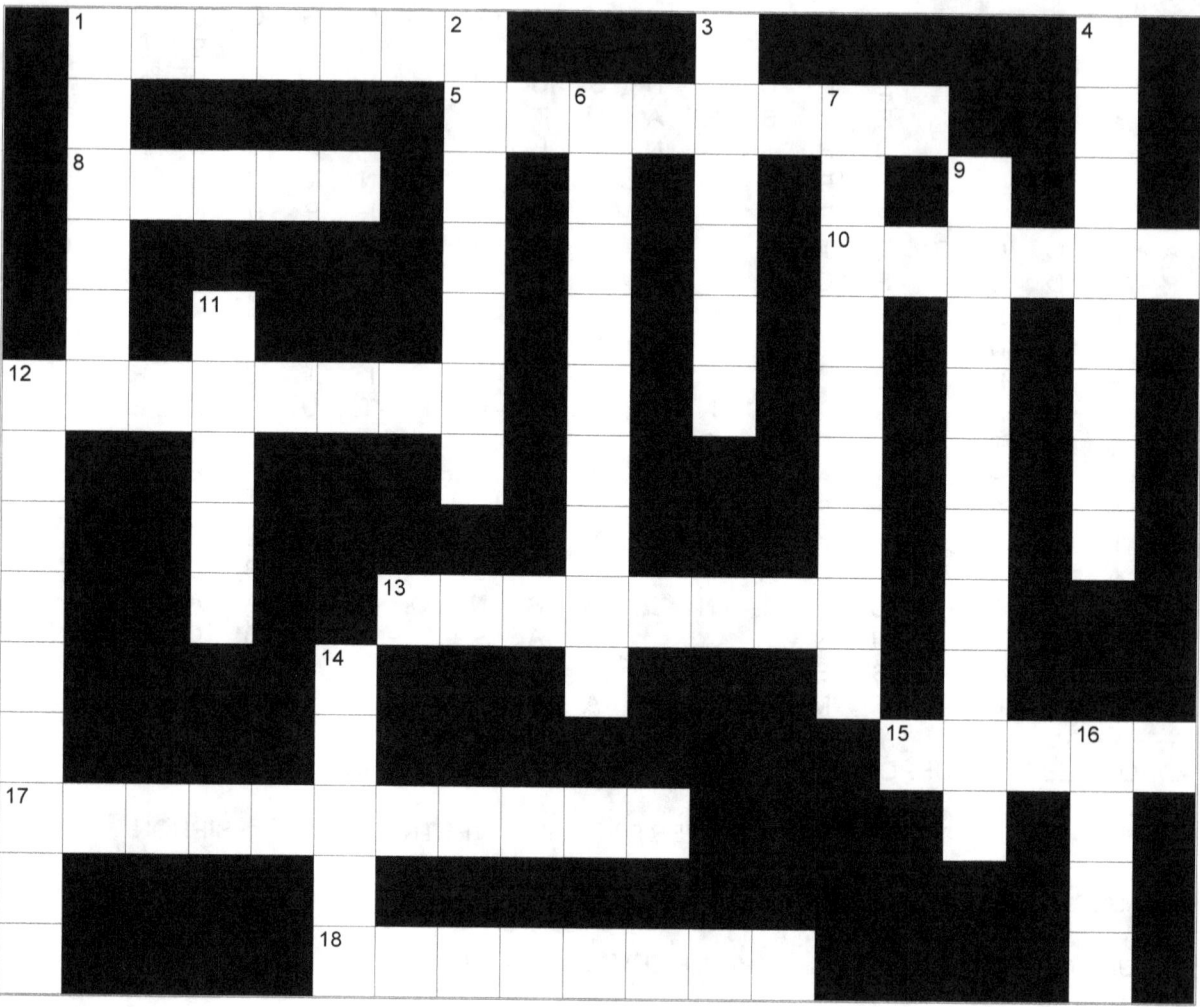

Across
1. Physical or moral strength to resist or withstand illness, fatigue, or hardship; endurance
5. Capable of being done, effected, or accomplished
8. Characterized by a hypocritical concern with virtue or religious devotion
10. Lengths of thread or yarn wound in loose, long coils
12. In between period of time
13. Shrunk back, as in fear or repugnance
15. Unable to move or act
17. Inflammation of the membrane surrounding the abdominal cavity
18. A small dagger with a slender, tapering blade

Down
1. Pipe or tube to draw off or convey liquid
2. In a friendly, cordial manner
3. Small tool for boring holes
4. Division of the High Court of Justice of Great Britain
6. Mechanical figure; robot
7. Weariness of body or mind from strain; lack of energy
9. Demeanor; conduct; behavior
11. Wharf; landing pier
12. Made or done without previous preparation
14. Indefinitely long periods of time
16. Thick and firm outer coat or covering

And Then There Were None Vocabulary Crossword 1 Answer Key

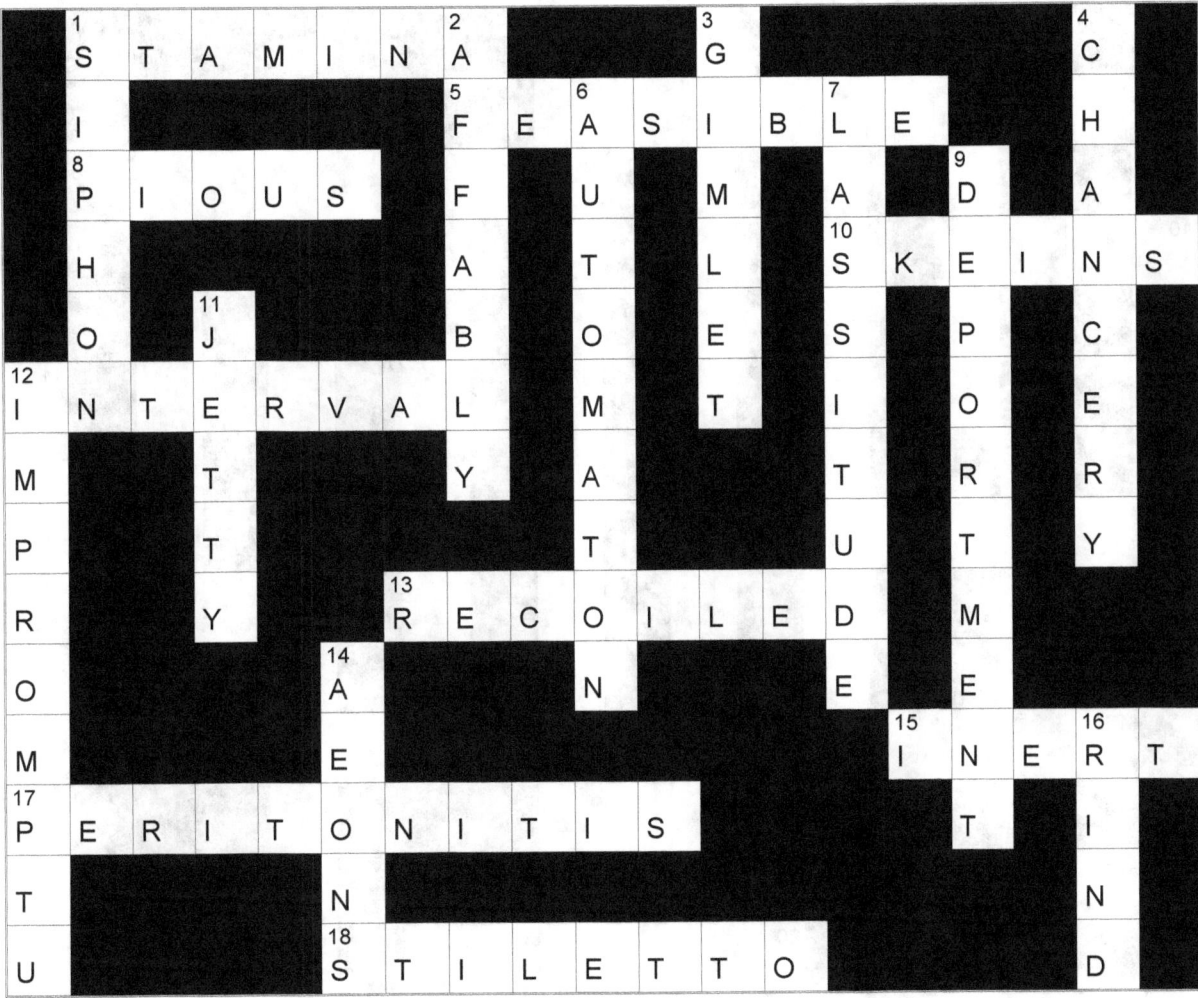

Across
1. Physical or moral strength to resist or withstand illness, fatigue, or hardship; endurance
5. Capable of being done, effected, or accomplished
8. Characterized by a hypocritical concern with virtue or religious devotion
10. Lengths of thread or yarn wound in loose, long coils
12. In between period of time
13. Shrunk back, as in fear or repugnance
15. Unable to move or act
17. Inflammation of the membrane surrounding the abdominal cavity
18. A small dagger with a slender, tapering blade

Down
1. Pipe or tube to draw off or convey liquid
2. In a friendly, cordial manner
3. Small tool for boring holes
4. Division of the High Court of Justice of Great Britain
6. Mechanical figure; robot
7. Weariness of body or mind from strain; lack of energy
9. Demeanor; conduct; behavior
11. Wharf; landing pier
12. Made or done without previous preparation
14. Indefinitely long periods of time
16. Thick and firm outer coat or covering

And Then There Were None Vocabulary Crossword 2

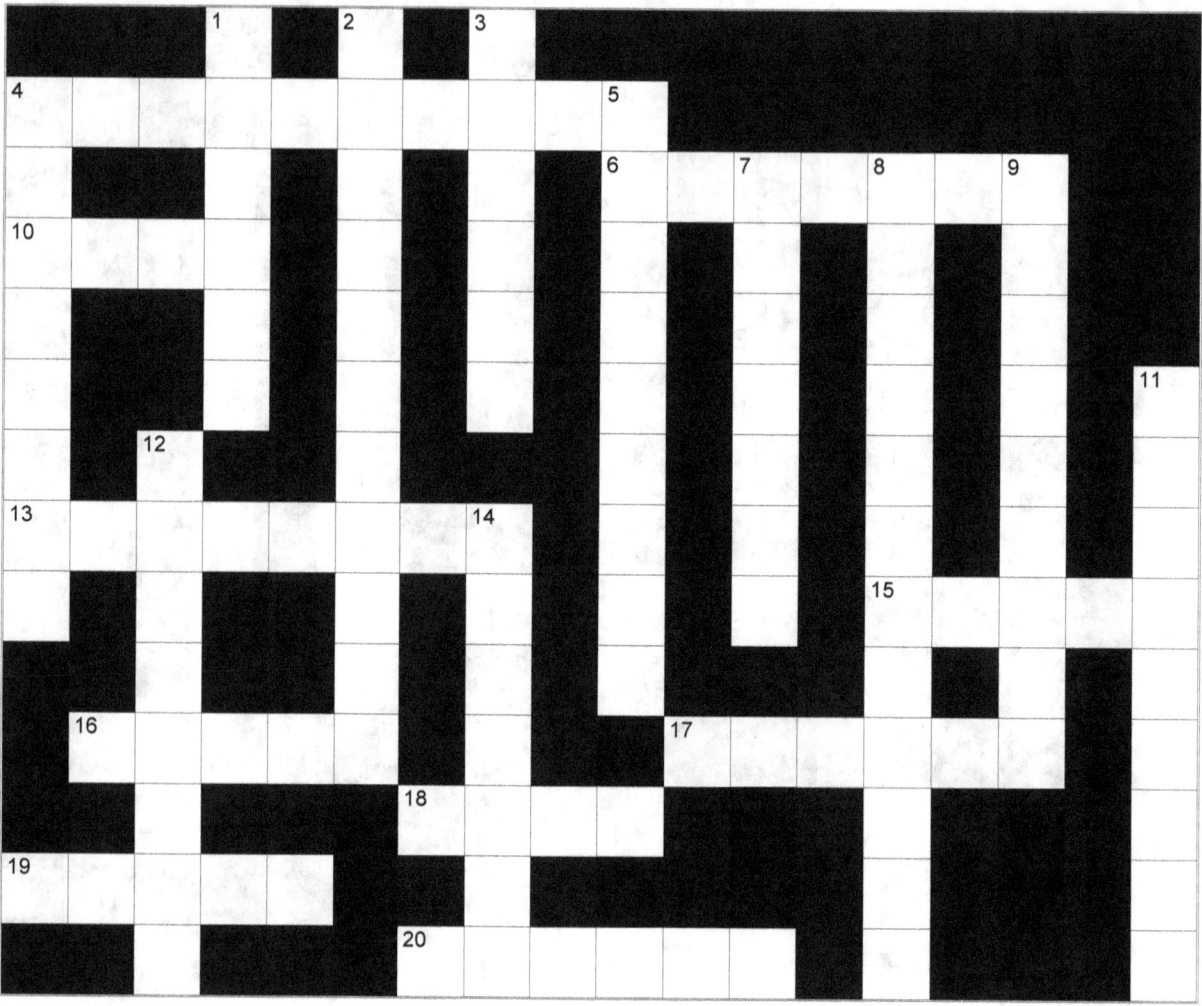

Across
4. Reflecting on over and over again; turning a matter over in the mind
6. Investigation made by a coroner into the cause of a death
10. Anything that covers, shrouds, or overspreads, esp. with darkness or gloom
13. Private or secret meeting
15. Indefinitely long periods of time
16. Wharf; landing pier
17. Lengths of thread or yarn wound in loose, long coils
18. Thick and firm outer coat or covering
19. Unable to move or act
20. Gift of property or money through a will; a bequest

Down
1. Small tool for boring holes
2. Peaceably, mildly, calmly, or quietly
3. Pipe or tube to draw off or convey liquid
4. Find fault with; blame; censure
5. Dizziness
7. Discharge or release from life
8. Sudden, short exclamations, especially brief pious utterances or prayers
9. Holding fast; characterized by keeping a firm hold
11. Weariness of body or mind from strain; lack of energy
12. Disregarded; ignored
14. Hard, non-resilient rubber formed by vulcanizing natural rubber

And Then There Were None Vocabulary Crossword 2 Answer Key

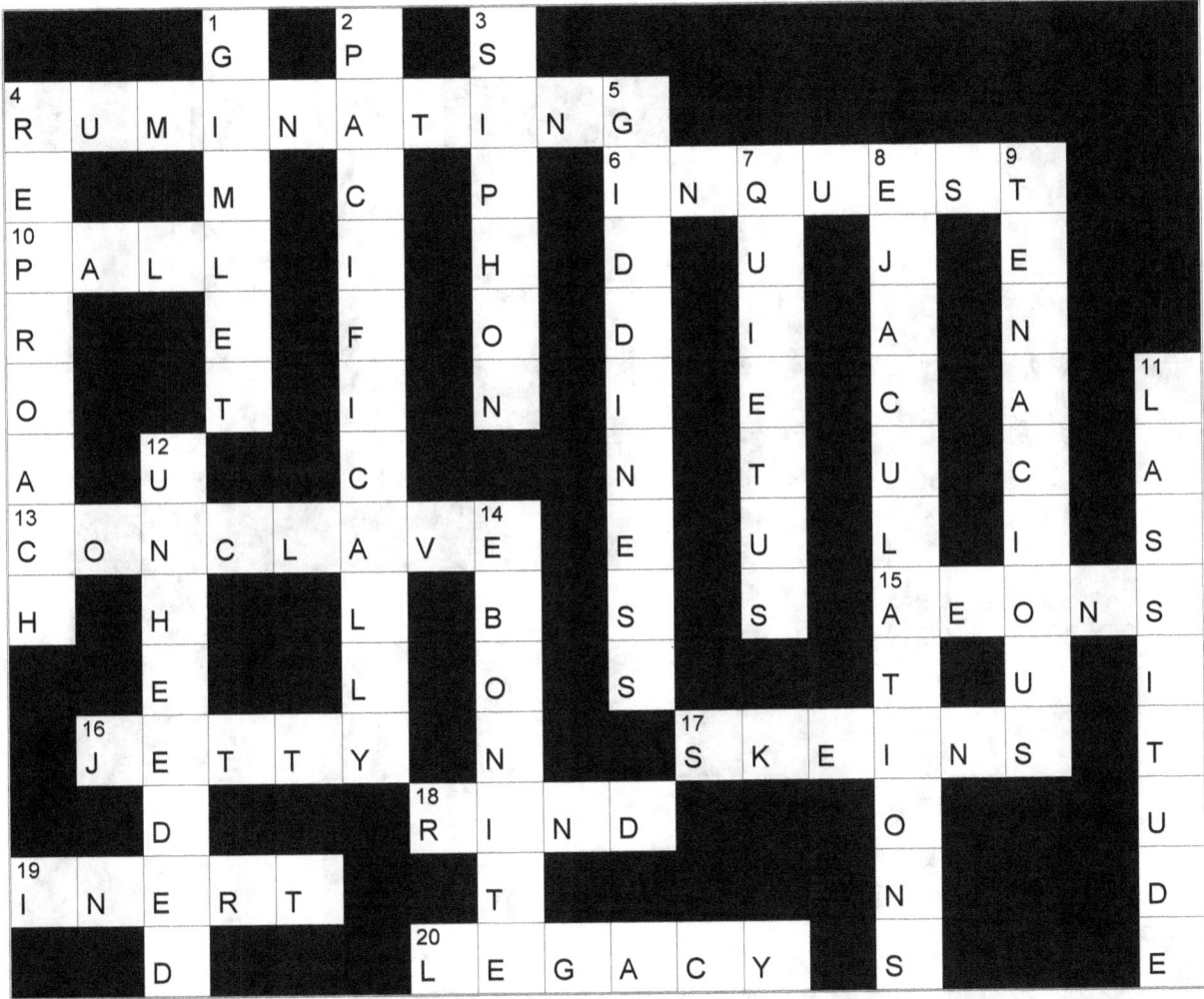

Across
4. Reflecting on over and over again; turning a matter over in the mind
6. Investigation made by a coroner into the cause of a death
10. Anything that covers, shrouds, or overspreads, esp. with darkness or gloom
13. Private or secret meeting
15. Indefinitely long periods of time
16. Wharf; landing pier
17. Lengths of thread or yarn wound in loose, long coils
18. Thick and firm outer coat or covering
19. Unable to move or act
20. Gift of property or money through a will; a bequest

Down
1. Small tool for boring holes
2. Peaceably, mildly, calmly, or quietly
3. Pipe or tube to draw off or convey liquid
4. Find fault with; blame; censure
5. Dizziness
7. Discharge or release from life
8. Sudden, short exclamations, especially brief pious utterances or prayers
9. Holding fast; characterized by keeping a firm hold
11. Weariness of body or mind from strain; lack of energy
12. Disregarded; ignored
14. Hard, non-resilient rubber formed by vulcanizing natural rubber

And Then There Were None Vocabulary Crossword 3

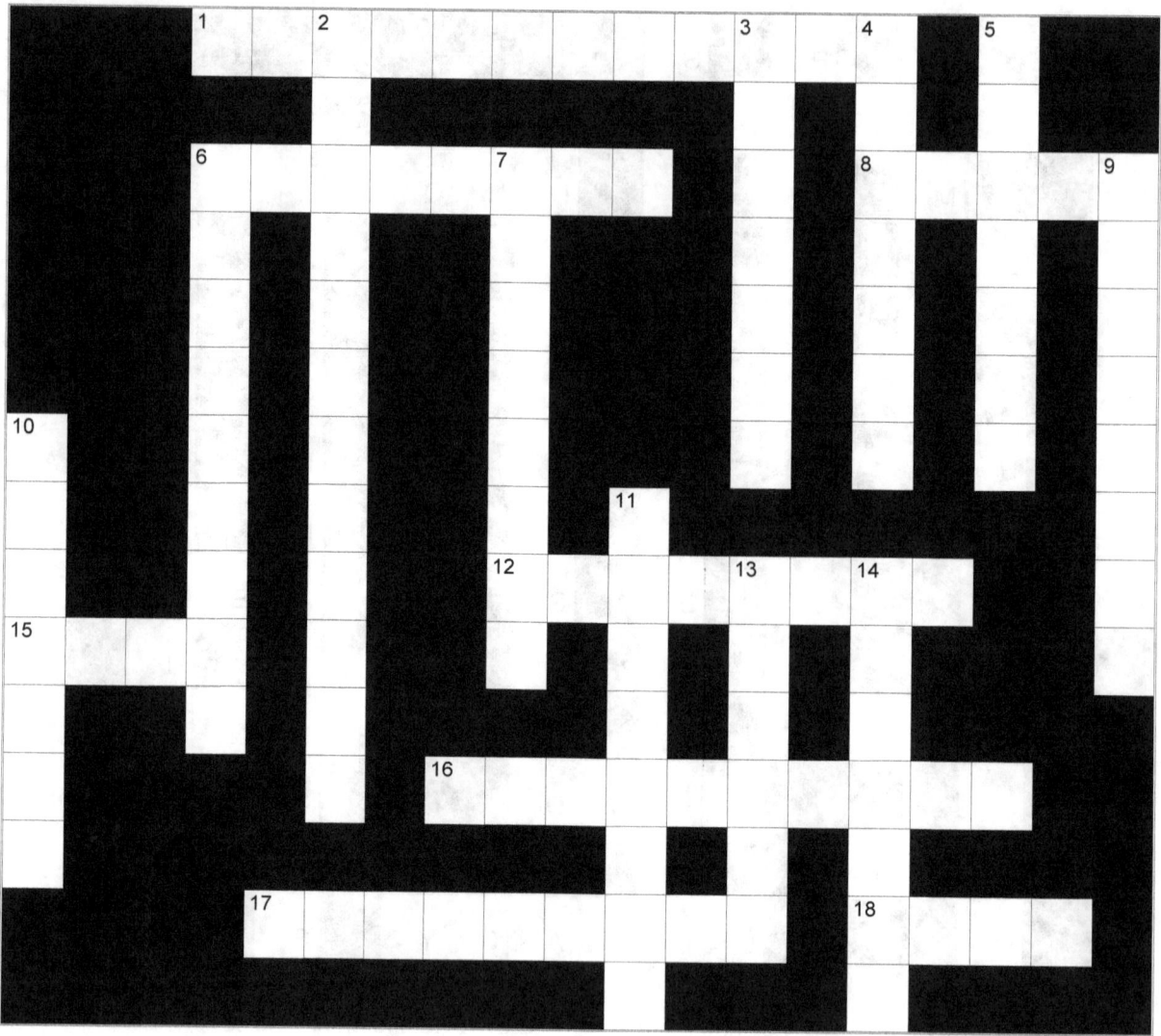

Across
1. Sudden, short exclamations, especially brief pious utterances or prayers
6. Crudely or irregularly fashioned verse, often of a humorous or burlesque nature
8. Indefinitely long periods of time
12. Private or secret meeting
15. Anything that covers, shrouds, or overspreads, esp. with darkness or gloom
16. Unoccupied; not leased to or occupied by a tenant
17. Having a slanting or sloping direction, course, or position
18. Thick and firm outer coat or covering

Down
2. Sharp corners; angular outlines
3. Heavy, water-resistant fabric
4. Physical or moral strength to resist or withstand illness, fatigue, or hardship; endurance
5. Hard, non-resilient rubber formed by vulcanizing natural rubber
6. In a doubtful manner
7. Find fault with; blame; censure
9. In a calm, peaceful, or tranquil manner
10. Mysterious in meaning; puzzling; ambiguous
11. Disregarded; ignored
13. Gift of property or money through a will; a bequest
14. Undertaking involving uncertainty as to the outcome

And Then There Were None Vocabulary Crossword 3 Answer Key

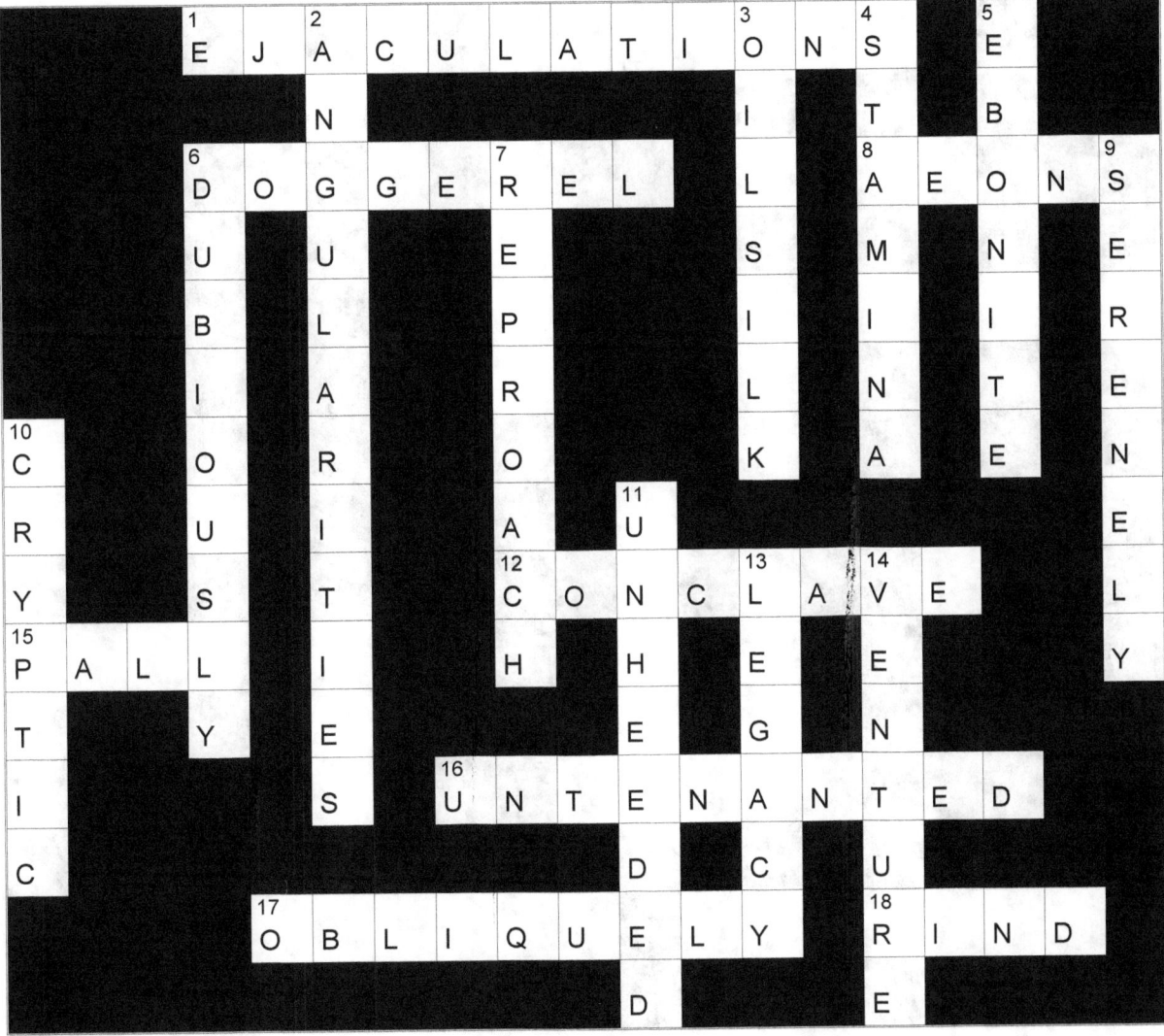

Across
1. Sudden, short exclamations, especially brief pious utterances or prayers
6. Crudely or irregularly fashioned verse, often of a humorous or burlesque nature
8. Indefinitely long periods of time
12. Private or secret meeting
15. Anything that covers, shrouds, or overspreads, esp. with darkness or gloom
16. Unoccupied; not leased to or occupied by a tenant
17. Having a slanting or sloping direction, course, or position
18. Thick and firm outer coat or covering

Down
2. Sharp corners; angular outlines
3. Heavy, water-resistant fabric
4. Physical or moral strength to resist or withstand illness, fatigue, or hardship; endurance
5. Hard, non-resilient rubber formed by vulcanizing natural rubber
6. In a doubtful manner
7. Find fault with; blame; censure
9. In a calm, peaceful, or tranquil manner
10. Mysterious in meaning; puzzling; ambiguous
11. Disregarded; ignored
13. Gift of property or money through a will; a bequest
14. Undertaking involving uncertainty as to the outcome

And Then There Were None Vocabulary Crossword 4

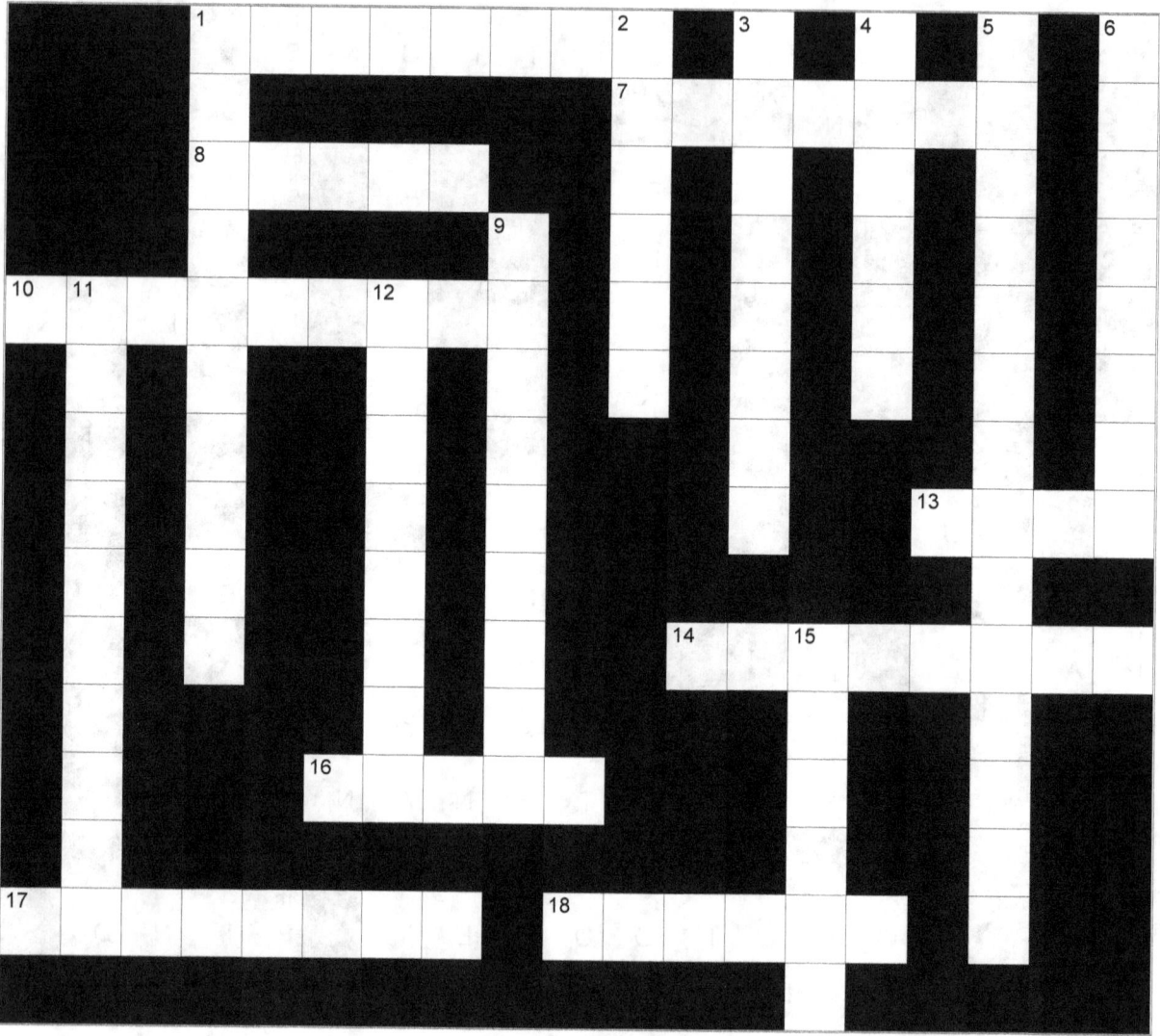

Across
1. Crudely or irregularly fashioned verse, often of a humorous or burlesque nature
7. Hard, non-resilient rubber formed by vulcanizing natural rubber
8. Characterized by a hypocritical concern with virtue or religious devotion
10. Made or done without previous preparation
13. Thick and firm outer coat or covering
14. State of being completely forgotten or unknown
16. Indefinitely long periods of time
17. Physical or bodily structure; appearance
18. Small tool for boring holes

Down
1. Demeanor; conduct; behavior
2. Gift of property or money through a will; a bequest
3. Secretly; in a concealed manner
4. Pipe or tube to draw off or convey liquid
5. Appearance or semblance of truth; likelihood; probability
6. Spread through or over, as with liquid, color, or light
9. Mechanical figure; robot
11. Raincoat
12. False showing
15. Room or place where food is stored; pantry

And Then There Were None Vocabulary Crossword 4 Answer Key

Across
1. Crudely or irregularly fashioned verse, often of a humorous or burlesque nature
7. Hard, non-resilient rubber formed by vulcanizing natural rubber
8. Characterized by a hypocritical concern with virtue or religious devotion
10. Made or done without previous preparation
13. Thick and firm outer coat or covering
14. State of being completely forgotten or unknown
16. Indefinitely long periods of time
17. Physical or bodily structure; appearance
18. Small tool for boring holes

Down
1. Demeanor; conduct; behavior
2. Gift of property or money through a will; a bequest
3. Secretly; in a concealed manner
4. Pipe or tube to draw off or convey liquid
5. Appearance or semblance of truth; likelihood; probability
6. Spread through or over, as with liquid, color, or light
9. Mechanical figure; robot
11. Raincoat
12. False showing
15. Room or place where food is stored; pantry

And Then There Were None Vocabulary Juggle Letters 1

1. SDUNUOETPS = 1. _____
   Causing amazement; astounding; marvelous

2. YCCNHRAE = 2. _____
   Division of the High Court of Justice of Great Britain

3. DITIECLUOS = 3. _____
   Attitude expressing excessive attentiveness

4. CAABRTTS = 4. _____
   Theoretical; not applied or practical

5. RMOPUIPTM = 5. _____
   Made or done without previous preparation

6. KSESNI = 6. _____
   Lengths of thread or yarn wound in loose, long coils

7. LAPL = 7. _____
   Anything that covers, shrouds, or overspreads, esp. with darkness or gloom

8. REEECNTP = 8. _____
   False showing

9. NNINITOALCI = 9. _____
   Disposition or bent, esp. of the mind or will; a liking or preference

10. RRLEDA = 10. _____
    Room or place where food is stored; pantry

11. OUNCNIOSU = 11. _____
    Harmless

12. NPOHSI = 12. _____
    Pipe or tube to draw off or convey liquid

13. ERTHOIHT = 13. _____
    Up to this time; until now

14. NISJCLATOEUA = 14. _____
    Sudden, short exclamations, especially brief pious utterances or prayers

And Then There Were None Vocabulary Juggle Letters 1 Answer Key

1. SDUNUOETPS = 1. STUPENDOUS
   Causing amazement; astounding; marvelous

2. YCCNHRAE = 2. CHANCERY
   Division of the High Court of Justice of Great Britain

3. DITIECLUOS = 3. SOLICITUDE
   Attitude expressing excessive attentiveness

4. CAABRTTS = 4. ABSTRACT
   Theoretical; not applied or practical

5. RMOPUIPTM = 5. IMPROMPTU
   Made or done without previous preparation

6. KSESNI = 6. SKEINS
   Lengths of thread or yarn wound in loose, long coils

7. LAPL = 7. PALL
   Anything that covers, shrouds, or overspreads, esp. with darkness or gloom

8. REEECNTP = 8. PRETENCE
   False showing

9. NNINITOALCI = 9. INCLINATION
   Disposition or bent, esp. of the mind or will; a liking or preference

10. RRLEDA = 10. LARDER
    Room or place where food is stored; pantry

11. OUNCNIOSU = 11. INNOCUOUS
    Harmless

12. NPOHSI = 12. SIPHON
    Pipe or tube to draw off or convey liquid

13. ERTHOIHT = 13. HITHERTO
    Up to this time; until now

14. NISJCLATOEUA = 14. EJACULATIONS
    Sudden, short exclamations, especially brief pious utterances or prayers

And Then There Were None Vocabulary Juggle Letters 2

1. DERCNUORC = 1. _____
   Was of the same opinion; agreed

2. NTEVERU = 2. _____
   Undertaking involving uncertainty as to the outcome

3. KLLOSII = 3. _____
   Heavy, water-resistant fabric

4. ETEYVUSLLRAIP = 4. _____
   Of the highest kind, quality, or order; surpassing all else or others

5. NEOERMTTPD = 5. _____
   Demeanor; conduct; behavior

6. ESFBIELA = 6. _____
   Capable of being done, effected, or accomplished

7. ARRDICEBDA = 7. _____
   Blocked with a defensive barrier

8. CATTRBAS = 8. _____
   Theoretical; not applied or practical

9. NSHIPO = 9. _____
   Pipe or tube to draw off or convey liquid

10. NGNIRAMUIT =10. _____
    Reflecting on over and over again; turning a matter over in the mind

11. DEUDEENH =11. _____
    Disregarded; ignored

12. LPTROE =12. _____
    Gasoline

13. RRELAD =13. _____
    Room or place where food is stored; pantry

14. NCERINIIATMOR =14. _____
    Act of accusing in return

And Then There Were None Vocabulary Juggle Letters 2 Answer Key

1. DERCNUORC = 1. CONCURRED
   Was of the same opinion; agreed

2. NTEVERU = 2. VENTURE
   Undertaking involving uncertainty as to the outcome

3. KLLOSII = 3. OILSILK
   Heavy, water-resistant fabric

4. ETEYVUSLLRAIP = 4. SUPERLATIVELY
   Of the highest kind, quality, or order; surpassing all else or others

5. NEOERMTTPD = 5. DEPORTMENT
   Demeanor; conduct; behavior

6. ESFBIELA = 6. FEASIBLE
   Capable of being done, effected, or accomplished

7. ARRDICEBDA = 7. BARRICADED
   Blocked with a defensive barrier

8. CATTRBAS = 8. ABSTRACT
   Theoretical; not applied or practical

9. NSHIPO = 9. SIPHON
   Pipe or tube to draw off or convey liquid

10. NGNIRAMUIT = 10. RUMINATING
    Reflecting on over and over again; turning a matter over in the mind

11. DEUDEENH = 11. UNHEEDED
    Disregarded; ignored

12. LPTROE = 12. PETROL
    Gasoline

13. RRELAD = 13. LARDER
    Room or place where food is stored; pantry

14. NCERINIIATMOR = 14. RECRIMINATION
    Act of accusing in return

And Then There Were None Vocabulary Juggle Letters 3

1. LNYEAETLVOML = 1. _____
   In an evil, harmful, or injurious manner

2. EROELDGG = 2. _____
   Crudely or irregularly fashioned verse, often of a humorous or burlesque nature

3. ELRDMEACB = 3. _____
   Climbed with difficulty, especially on all fours

4. ISOINTRIEPT = 4. _____
   Inflammation of the membrane surrounding the abdominal cavity

5. TMLEGI = 5. _____
   Small tool for boring holes

6. OLSTEITT = 6. _____
   A small dagger with a slender, tapering blade

7. ERDRCDAAIB = 7. _____
   Blocked with a defensive barrier

8. UCEAONNCTNE = 8. _____
   Look or expression of the face

9. PEHROARC = 9. _____
   Find fault with; blame; censure

10. NCLNIIANTIO = 10. _____
    Disposition or bent, esp. of the mind or will; a liking or preference

11. DUFSFEUS = 11. _____
    Spread through or over, as with liquid, color, or light

12. OMRUPMTPI = 12. _____
    Made or done without previous preparation

13. TUSNLIJECAOA = 13. _____
    Sudden, short exclamations, especially brief pious utterances or prayers

14. EOLTPR = 14. _____
    Gasoline

And Then There Were None Vocabulary Juggle Letters 3 Answer Key

1. LNYEAETLVOML = 1. MALEVOLENTLY
   In an evil, harmful, or injurious manner

2. EROELDGG = 2. DOGGEREL
   Crudely or irregularly fashioned verse, often of a humorous or burlesque nature

3. ELRDMEACB = 3. CLAMBERED
   Climbed with difficulty, especially on all fours

4. ISOINTRIEPT = 4. PERITONITIS
   Inflammation of the membrane surrounding the abdominal cavity

5. TMLEGI = 5. GIMLET
   Small tool for boring holes

6. OLSTEITT = 6. STILETTO
   A small dagger with a slender, tapering blade

7. ERDRCDAAIB = 7. BARRICADED
   Blocked with a defensive barrier

8. UCEAONNCTNE = 8. COUNTENANCE
   Look or expression of the face

9. PEHROARC = 9. REPROACH
   Find fault with; blame; censure

10. NCLNIIANTIO =10. INCLINATION
    Disposition or bent, esp. of the mind or will; a liking or preference

11. DUFSFEUS =11. SUFFUSED
    Spread through or over, as with liquid, color, or light

12. OMRUPMTPI =12. IMPROMPTU
    Made or done without previous preparation

13. TUSNLIJECAOA =13. EJACULATIONS
    Sudden, short exclamations, especially brief pious utterances or prayers

14. EOLTPR =14. PETROL
    Gasoline

And Then There Were None Vocabulary Juggle Letters 4

1. METILG = 1. _____
   Small tool for boring holes

2. GYCAIAST = 2. _____
   Acuteness of mental discernment and soundness of judgment

3. IGNSDIESD = 3. _____
   Dizziness

4. CBATRATS = 4. _____
   Theoretical; not applied or practical

5. UERTAYLSEIVPL = 5. _____
   Of the highest kind, quality, or order; surpassing all else or others

6. NORRGMCIA = 6. _____
   Smoky-yellow to dark brown or black variety of quartz, used as a gem stone

7. ECABLDMER = 7. _____
   Climbed with difficulty, especially on all fours

8. TAIEOSDNRS = 8. _____
   Expertise or nimbleness in the use of the hands or body

9. TEPEECRN = 9. _____
   False showing

10. QPHUSEIY =10. _____
    Physical or bodily structure; appearance

11. ITEVLRUIEIDIMS =11. _____
    Appearance or semblance of truth; likelihood; probability

12. EIDERLAENTF =12. _____
    Showing regard or respect

13. RAERHCPO =13. _____
    Find fault with; blame; censure

14. PEERTNMDOT =14. _____
    Demeanor; conduct; behavior

And Then There Were None Vocabulary Juggle Letters 4 Answer Key

1. METILG = 1. GIMLET
   Small tool for boring holes

2. GYCAIAST = 2. SAGACITY
   Acuteness of mental discernment and soundness of judgment

3. IGNSDIESD = 3. GIDDINESS
   Dizziness

4. CBATRATS = 4. ABSTRACT
   Theoretical; not applied or practical

5. UERTAYLSEIVPL = 5. SUPERLATIVELY
   Of the highest kind, quality, or order; surpassing all else or others

6. NORRGMCIA = 6. CAIRNGORM
   Smoky-yellow to dark brown or black variety of quartz, used as a gem stone

7. ECABLDMER = 7. CLAMBERED
   Climbed with difficulty, especially on all fours

8. TAIEOSDNRS = 8. ADROITNESS
   Expertise or nimbleness in the use of the hands or body

9. TEPEECRN = 9. PRETENCE
   False showing

10. QPHUSEIY =10. PHYSIQUE
    Physical or bodily structure; appearance

11. ITEVLRUIEIDIMS =11. VERISIMILITUDE
    Appearance or semblance of truth; likelihood; probability

12. EIDERLAENTF =12. DEFERENTIAL
    Showing regard or respect

13. RAERHCPO =13. REPROACH
    Find fault with; blame; censure

14. PEERTNMDOT =14. DEPORTMENT
    Demeanor; conduct; behavior

ABHORRENT	Detestable; loathsome; hateful
ABSTRACT	Theoretical; not applied or practical
ADMONITORY	Serving to warn, especially to correct
ADROITNESS	Expertise or nimbleness in the use of the hands or body
AEONS	Indefinitely long periods of time
AFFABLY	In a friendly, cordial manner

AMPOULE	Sealed glass or plastic bulb containing solutions for hypodermic injection
ANGULARITIES	Sharp corners; angular outlines
ASPHYXIATION	Death by choking, smothering, or suffocating
AUTOMATON	Mechanical figure; robot
BARRICADED	Blocked with a defensive barrier
CAIRNGORM	Smoky-yellow to dark brown or black variety of quartz, used as a gem stone

CHANCERY	Division of the High Court of Justice of Great Britain
CLAMBERED	Climbed with difficulty, especially on all fours
CONCLAVE	Private or secret meeting
CONCURRED	Was of the same opinion; agreed
CONJURING	Affecting or influencing as if by invocation or a magic spell
COUNTENANCE	Look or expression of the face

COVERTLY	Secretly; in a concealed manner
CRYPTIC	Mysterious in meaning; puzzling; ambiguous
DEFERENTIAL	Showing regard or respect
DEPORTMENT	Demeanor; conduct; behavior
DESULTORY	Lacking in consistency or visible order; disconnected
DOGGEREL	Crudely or irregularly fashioned verse, often of a humorous or burlesque nature

DRAUGHT	Dose of liquid medicine
DUBIOUSLY	In a doubtful manner
EBONITE	Hard, non-resilient rubber formed by vulcanizing natural rubber
EJACULATIONS	Sudden, short exclamations, especially brief pious utterances or prayers
EXIGENCIES	Pressing or urgent situations
FEASIBLE	Capable of being done, effected, or accomplished

GIDDINESS	Dizziness
GIMLET	Small tool for boring holes
HELIOGRAPHING	Transmitting messages by reflecting sunlight
HITHERTO	Up to this time; until now
IMPROMPTU	Made or done without previous preparation
INCLINATION	Disposition or bent, esp. of the mind or will; a liking or preference

INDICTMENTS	Written statements charging a party with the commission of a crime
INERT	Unable to move or act
INEVITABILITY	Unable to be avoided, evaded, or escaped
INNOCUOUS	Harmless
INQUEST	Investigation made by a coroner into the cause of a death
INTERVAL	In between period of time

JETTY	Wharf; landing pier
LARDER	Room or place where food is stored; pantry
LASSITUDE	Weariness of body or mind from strain; lack of energy
LEGACY	Gift of property or money through a will; a bequest
MACKINTOSH	Raincoat
MALEVOLENTLY	In an evil, harmful, or injurious manner

MALICIOUS	Deliberately harmful or spiteful
OBLIQUELY	Having a slanting or sloping direction, course, or position
OBLIVION	State of being completely forgotten or unknown
OILSILK	Heavy, water-resistant fabric
PACIFICALLY	Peaceably, mildly, calmly, or quietly
PALL	Anything that covers, shrouds, or overspreads, esp. with darkness or gloom

PALPABLY	Plainly seen, heard, or perceived; obviously
PERITONITIS	Inflammation of the membrane surrounding the abdominal cavity
PETROL	Gasoline
PHYSIQUE	Physical or bodily structure; appearance
PIOUS	Characterized by a hypocritical concern with virtue or religious devotion
PRETENCE	False showing

PROBATIONER	Nurse in training who is undergoing a trial period
PROVISIONED	Provided a stock of necessary supplies, especially food
QUIETUS	Discharge or release from life
RECOILED	Shrunk back, as in fear or repugnance
RECONNAISSANCE	Search made for useful military information in the field
RECRIMINATION	Act of accusing in return

REPROACH	Find fault with; blame; censure
RIND	Thick and firm outer coat or covering
RUMINATING	Reflecting on over and over again; turning a matter over in the mind
SAGACITY	Acuteness of mental discernment and soundness of judgment
SERENELY	In a calm, peaceful, or tranquil manner
SIDEBOARD	Piece of dining room furniture having drawers and shelves for linens and tableware

SIPHON	Pipe or tube to draw off or convey liquid
SKEINS	Lengths of thread or yarn wound in loose, long coils
SOLICITUDE	Attitude expressing excessive attentiveness
STAMINA	Physical or moral strength to resist or withstand illness, fatigue, or hardship; endurance
STILETTO	A small dagger with a slender, tapering blade
STUPENDOUS	Causing amazement; astounding; marvelous

SUBSEQUENT	Occurring or coming later or after
SUFFUSED	Spread through or over, as with liquid, color, or light
SUPERLATIVELY	Of the highest kind, quality, or order; surpassing all else or others
TENACIOUS	Holding fast; characterized by keeping a firm hold
UNHEEDED	Disregarded; ignored
UNOBTRUSIVELY	In a manner that is not undesirably noticeable or blatant

UNTENANTED	Unoccupied; not leased to or occupied by a tenant
VENTURE	Undertaking involving uncertainty as to the outcome
VERISIMILITUDE	Appearance or semblance of truth; likelihood; probability

And Then There Were None Vocabulary

ANGULARITIES	CONCURRED	CRYPTIC	GIDDINESS	DUBIOUSLY
HITHERTO	RIND	CLAMBERED	PROVISIONED	PETROL
SAGACITY	CHANCERY	FREE SPACE	MALICIOUS	HELIOGRAPHING
INDICTMENTS	LASSITUDE	EJACULATIONS	INQUEST	COVERTLY
STAMINA	AUTOMATON	LEGACY	RECOILED	UNHEEDED

And Then There Were None Vocabulary

RUMINATING	LARDER	RECONNAISSANCE	VENTURE	ADMONITORY
CONJURING	UNOBTRUSIVELY	PALL	PALPABLY	OILSILK
AFFABLY	BARRICADED	FREE SPACE	DOGGEREL	ASPHYXIATION
COUNTENANCE	JETTY	INCLINATION	CAIRNGORM	ABHORRENT
CONCLAVE	PRETENCE	MACKINTOSH	SIDEBOARD	TENACIOUS

And Then There Were None Vocabulary

ABSTRACT	SIDEBOARD	ADMONITORY	CAIRNGORM	SUBSEQUENT
PROBATIONER	RECONNAISSANCE	HITHERTO	OILSILK	LARDER
STAMINA	CLAMBERED	FREE SPACE	VERISIMILITUDE	SAGACITY
JETTY	ANGULARITIES	PHYSIQUE	INTERVAL	RECOILED
LASSITUDE	PERITONITIS	CONJURING	TENACIOUS	REPROACH

And Then There Were None Vocabulary

PALL	DRAUGHT	RUMINATING	SUFFUSED	AUTOMATON
UNTENANTED	AMPOULE	COVERTLY	PROVISIONED	RIND
DESULTORY	CONCLAVE	FREE SPACE	UNOBTRUSIVELY	BARRICADED
DEFERENTIAL	MALEVOLENTLY	PALPABLY	SOLICITUDE	INQUEST
PIOUS	COUNTENANCE	EBONITE	PACIFICALLY	STUPENDOUS

And Then There Were None Vocabulary

SERENELY	CONCURRED	PETROL	DESULTORY	ADROITNESS
CLAMBERED	QUIETUS	GIDDINESS	LASSITUDE	GIMLET
IMPROMPTU	CHANCERY	FREE SPACE	AMPOULE	ANGULARITIES
MACKINTOSH	RUMINATING	CRYPTIC	SIPHON	PACIFICALLY
CAIRNGORM	ABHORRENT	PALL	ASPHYXIATION	SOLICITUDE

And Then There Were None Vocabulary

MALICIOUS	INCLINATION	SUFFUSED	ADMONITORY	DEPORTMENT
PRETENCE	DEFERENTIAL	CONCLAVE	INEVITABILITY	UNOBTRUSIVELY
INERT	INNOCUOUS	FREE SPACE	INDICTMENTS	VENTURE
INQUEST	PALPABLY	PROBATIONER	PROVISIONED	EBONITE
ABSTRACT	AUTOMATON	VERISIMILITUDE	OILSILK	RIND

And Then There Were None Vocabulary

EXIGENCIES	AEONS	IMPROMPTU	CONCLAVE	FEASIBLE
DEFERENTIAL	HITHERTO	SKEINS	PRETENCE	SUBSEQUENT
PACIFICALLY	CAIRNGORM	FREE SPACE	DOGGEREL	RECONNAISSANCE
DRAUGHT	PHYSIQUE	PETROL	VENTURE	AFFABLY
MACKINTOSH	ADMONITORY	HELIOGRAPHING	SAGACITY	OILSILK

And Then There Were None Vocabulary

SUFFUSED	JETTY	STILETTO	ADROITNESS	GIDDINESS
STUPENDOUS	QUIETUS	ABSTRACT	SIDEBOARD	STAMINA
SIPHON	COUNTENANCE	FREE SPACE	INDICTMENTS	UNOBTRUSIVELY
ASPHYXIATION	COVERTLY	AUTOMATON	SUPERLATIVELY	SERENELY
MALICIOUS	CONCURRED	VERISIMILITUDE	EBONITE	CRYPTIC

And Then There Were None Vocabulary

STILETTO	SUPERLATIVELY	ASPHYXIATION	LASSITUDE	AMPOULE
ADROITNESS	DOGGEREL	UNOBTRUSIVELY	MALICIOUS	VENTURE
COUNTENANCE	SKEINS	FREE SPACE	CONCLAVE	PACIFICALLY
PHYSIQUE	RIND	IMPROMPTU	INTERVAL	CONJURING
PETROL	FEASIBLE	INNOCUOUS	SIDEBOARD	OBLIVION

And Then There Were None Vocabulary

MALEVOLENTLY	HELIOGRAPHING	EXIGENCIES	RUMINATING	EJACULATIONS
INCLINATION	UNHEEDED	LARDER	OBLIQUELY	SUBSEQUENT
UNTENANTED	STUPENDOUS	FREE SPACE	DEPORTMENT	AFFABLY
MACKINTOSH	CONCURRED	RECONNAISSANCE	CLAMBERED	AUTOMATON
AEONS	SAGACITY	RECRIMINATION	JETTY	SUFFUSED

And Then There Were None Vocabulary

RECOILED	UNHEEDED	ADMONITORY	DESULTORY	ASPHYXIATION
PERITONITIS	SUFFUSED	PETROL	COVERTLY	SUBSEQUENT
MALICIOUS	CHANCERY	FREE SPACE	INQUEST	SUPERLATIVELY
LARDER	SAGACITY	SIPHON	SERENELY	DUBIOUSLY
TENACIOUS	CONCLAVE	RIND	PIOUS	MACKINTOSH

And Then There Were None Vocabulary

CONCURRED	STUPENDOUS	AEONS	IMPROMPTU	ABSTRACT
PACIFICALLY	DOGGEREL	LEGACY	CONJURING	UNOBTRUSIVELY
QUIETUS	STILETTO	FREE SPACE	VERISIMILITUDE	PROVISIONED
UNTENANTED	GIMLET	PALPABLY	SOLICITUDE	PROBATIONER
INCLINATION	STAMINA	REPROACH	INTERVAL	RECRIMINATION

And Then There Were None Vocabulary

GIMLET	LARDER	CONJURING	HITHERTO	INEVITABILITY
COUNTENANCE	SUBSEQUENT	OBLIVION	OBLIQUELY	RECONNAISSANCE
FEASIBLE	ANGULARITIES	FREE SPACE	INTERVAL	EBONITE
INNOCUOUS	RIND	UNOBTRUSIVELY	RECRIMINATION	IMPROMPTU
PALPABLY	DEPORTMENT	QUIETUS	VERISIMILITUDE	HELIOGRAPHING

And Then There Were None Vocabulary

CLAMBERED	INQUEST	RUMINATING	PALL	PRETENCE
DRAUGHT	SOLICITUDE	ABSTRACT	PERITONITIS	SAGACITY
STAMINA	DOGGEREL	FREE SPACE	DUBIOUSLY	OILSILK
UNHEEDED	PACIFICALLY	STILETTO	JETTY	ASPHYXIATION
CRYPTIC	UNTENANTED	ADMONITORY	REPROACH	AUTOMATON

And Then There Were None Vocabulary

CRYPTIC	TENACIOUS	INQUEST	GIMLET	PACIFICALLY
EXIGENCIES	LASSITUDE	ANGULARITIES	ABHORRENT	AEONS
SAGACITY	PHYSIQUE	FREE SPACE	INDICTMENTS	AMPOULE
RECONNAISSANCE	MACKINTOSH	FEASIBLE	PROVISIONED	AUTOMATON
CAIRNGORM	ADMONITORY	SKEINS	UNTENANTED	ABSTRACT

And Then There Were None Vocabulary

RUMINATING	HITHERTO	HELIOGRAPHING	INERT	COVERTLY
LEGACY	GIDDINESS	EBONITE	DRAUGHT	DEFERENTIAL
PROBATIONER	COUNTENANCE	FREE SPACE	SIDEBOARD	PERITONITIS
VENTURE	EJACULATIONS	RIND	SUPERLATIVELY	INTERVAL
CONJURING	UNHEEDED	CHANCERY	BARRICADED	PETROL

And Then There Were None Vocabulary

RECOILED	CONJURING	EXIGENCIES	PALL	EBONITE
SIDEBOARD	OILSILK	ANGULARITIES	SKEINS	PROBATIONER
UNHEEDED	RECONNAISSANCE	FREE SPACE	OBLIVION	HELIOGRAPHING
QUIETUS	AEONS	CONCURRED	FEASIBLE	CHANCERY
PHYSIQUE	DOGGEREL	DESULTORY	SERENELY	OBLIQUELY

And Then There Were None Vocabulary

DEPORTMENT	EJACULATIONS	INERT	PETROL	MACKINTOSH
REPROACH	CONCLAVE	PALPABLY	ABSTRACT	JETTY
CAIRNGORM	TENACIOUS	FREE SPACE	RECRIMINATION	SUBSEQUENT
STAMINA	LARDER	MALEVOLENTLY	MALICIOUS	CLAMBERED
PRETENCE	INEVITABILITY	STUPENDOUS	RIND	RUMINATING

And Then There Were None Vocabulary

AUTOMATON	STILETTO	PRETENCE	SERENELY	DEPORTMENT
RECRIMINATION	PERITONITIS	ANGULARITIES	ADROITNESS	GIMLET
AMPOULE	EXIGENCIES	FREE SPACE	INQUEST	OBLIVION
LASSITUDE	INEVITABILITY	EJACULATIONS	STUPENDOUS	HELIOGRAPHING
SIPHON	SUBSEQUENT	EBONITE	UNHEEDED	CRYPTIC

And Then There Were None Vocabulary

DUBIOUSLY	PROVISIONED	PROBATIONER	AFFABLY	CONCURRED
MALEVOLENTLY	DEFERENTIAL	INERT	ASPHYXIATION	SUPERLATIVELY
MALICIOUS	INTERVAL	FREE SPACE	CONJURING	AEONS
LARDER	LEGACY	SAGACITY	ADMONITORY	SUFFUSED
RIND	VERISIMILITUDE	COUNTENANCE	FEASIBLE	PALL

And Then There Were None Vocabulary

JETTY	REPROACH	UNTENANTED	COUNTENANCE	AMPOULE
UNOBTRUSIVELY	SERENELY	RECRIMINATION	SUBSEQUENT	PALL
MALICIOUS	CONCLAVE	FREE SPACE	GIMLET	STUPENDOUS
AFFABLY	LEGACY	CRYPTIC	RIND	IMPROMPTU
AEONS	QUIETUS	DEPORTMENT	ANGULARITIES	PRETENCE

And Then There Were None Vocabulary

RECONNAISSANCE	CAIRNGORM	EXIGENCIES	ADMONITORY	DEFERENTIAL
AUTOMATON	DUBIOUSLY	EBONITE	ASPHYXIATION	UNHEEDED
PROBATIONER	OBLIQUELY	FREE SPACE	PALPABLY	TENACIOUS
DESULTORY	SUFFUSED	SOLICITUDE	COVERTLY	SAGACITY
VENTURE	PETROL	FEASIBLE	PROVISIONED	SKEINS

And Then There Were None Vocabulary

SERENELY	PROBATIONER	SIPHON	BARRICADED	DUBIOUSLY
CRYPTIC	STAMINA	PROVISIONED	INQUEST	CLAMBERED
OBLIVION	DRAUGHT	FREE SPACE	INCLINATION	SUPERLATIVELY
SUBSEQUENT	INERT	AUTOMATON	ADROITNESS	PRETENCE
GIMLET	TENACIOUS	INEVITABILITY	COUNTENANCE	INNOCUOUS

And Then There Were None Vocabulary

MACKINTOSH	OBLIQUELY	RUMINATING	ABSTRACT	CAIRNGORM
PHYSIQUE	ADMONITORY	GIDDINESS	UNHEEDED	ANGULARITIES
HITHERTO	OILSILK	FREE SPACE	DOGGEREL	ASPHYXIATION
VERISIMILITUDE	RECRIMINATION	CHANCERY	AEONS	RIND
UNOBTRUSIVELY	SIDEBOARD	SUFFUSED	EJACULATIONS	CONCLAVE

And Then There Were None Vocabulary

PETROL	OBLIQUELY	UNTENANTED	LARDER	PROBATIONER
PHYSIQUE	RECOILED	BARRICADED	STAMINA	GIDDINESS
JETTY	CRYPTIC	FREE SPACE	PACIFICALLY	SUBSEQUENT
MALEVOLENTLY	PIOUS	DUBIOUSLY	SUPERLATIVELY	SOLICITUDE
DRAUGHT	DEFERENTIAL	RIND	COUNTENANCE	ADMONITORY

And Then There Were None Vocabulary

INCLINATION	VENTURE	CONJURING	PALPABLY	AFFABLY
MACKINTOSH	ANGULARITIES	MALICIOUS	COVERTLY	SERENELY
RECONNAISSANCE	INDICTMENTS	FREE SPACE	PERITONITIS	DESULTORY
OBLIVION	EXIGENCIES	CHANCERY	CAIRNGORM	SIPHON
CONCLAVE	INTERVAL	AUTOMATON	CONCURRED	HITHERTO

And Then There Were None Vocabulary

PETROL	PALPABLY	TENACIOUS	LARDER	MACKINTOSH
DRAUGHT	GIMLET	CRYPTIC	MALEVOLENTLY	STUPENDOUS
IMPROMPTU	RECRIMINATION	FREE SPACE	INDICTMENTS	PACIFICALLY
DESULTORY	SUBSEQUENT	RIND	CONCURRED	DUBIOUSLY
SIPHON	REPROACH	SERENELY	HITHERTO	EXIGENCIES

And Then There Were None Vocabulary

CONJURING	STILETTO	DOGGEREL	UNTENANTED	SOLICITUDE
CLAMBERED	OBLIVION	JETTY	SKEINS	LEGACY
VENTURE	INTERVAL	FREE SPACE	DEFERENTIAL	INEVITABILITY
ABSTRACT	COUNTENANCE	ASPHYXIATION	SAGACITY	PERITONITIS
CONCLAVE	VERISIMILITUDE	INQUEST	SIDEBOARD	AEONS

And Then There Were None Vocabulary

INERT	TENACIOUS	PRETENCE	REPROACH	SERENELY
HITHERTO	PROVISIONED	UNTENANTED	ADMONITORY	IMPROMPTU
ASPHYXIATION	UNOBTRUSIVELY	FREE SPACE	MACKINTOSH	OBLIQUELY
HELIOGRAPHING	CHANCERY	CONCURRED	VENTURE	JETTY
PETROL	SKEINS	DESULTORY	ANGULARITIES	DUBIOUSLY

And Then There Were None Vocabulary

STAMINA	AEONS	AFFABLY	EJACULATIONS	RECONNAISSANCE
DEPORTMENT	CRYPTIC	FEASIBLE	LEGACY	SUPERLATIVELY
VERISIMILITUDE	SIPHON	FREE SPACE	INTERVAL	DRAUGHT
MALEVOLENTLY	QUIETUS	DEFERENTIAL	CAIRNGORM	LARDER
OBLIVION	LASSITUDE	PROBATIONER	RIND	GIMLET

And Then There Were None Vocabulary

COUNTENANCE	TENACIOUS	RIND	AUTOMATON	CONCLAVE
INCLINATION	SUBSEQUENT	CONJURING	CONCURRED	AFFABLY
CAIRNGORM	SOLICITUDE	FREE SPACE	UNHEEDED	IMPROMPTU
ASPHYXIATION	COVERTLY	SIPHON	GIMLET	PALL
PACIFICALLY	PHYSIQUE	INEVITABILITY	RUMINATING	SAGACITY

And Then There Were None Vocabulary

VERISIMILITUDE	FEASIBLE	QUIETUS	EJACULATIONS	ADROITNESS
INNOCUOUS	RECRIMINATION	STUPENDOUS	PETROL	SUPERLATIVELY
LASSITUDE	INTERVAL	FREE SPACE	PROVISIONED	STAMINA
LEGACY	PRETENCE	MACKINTOSH	ADMONITORY	SERENELY
CHANCERY	HELIOGRAPHING	SKEINS	SIDEBOARD	LARDER

www.ingramcontent.com/pod-product-compliance
Lightning Source LLC
Chambersburg PA
CBHW081452070526
44586CB00019B/2313